Strategies
for Writing

in the

SOCIAL STUDIES CLASSROOM

Kathleen Kopp

Strategies for Writing in the Social Studies Classroom
By Kathleen Kopp

Cover and Book Design: Hank McAfee
Book Layout: Mickey Cuthbertson

Library of Congress Cataloging-in-Publication Data
Kopp, Kathleen, 1967-
    Strategies for writing in the social studies classroom / Kathleen N. Kopp.
            p. cm.
        Includes bibliographical references.
        ISBN 978-1-936700-49-3 (pbk.)
    1. Social sciences--Study and teaching. 2. Language arts--Correlation with content
    subjects. 3. English language--Composition and exercises--Study and teaching. I. Title.
LB1584.K66 2012
372.83--dc23
                            2012000548

Maupin House publishes professional resources for K-12 educators. Contact us for
tailored, in-house training or to schedule an author for a workshop or conference.
Visit www.maupinhouse.com for free lesson plan downloads.

Maupin House *by*
capstone
professional

Maupin House Publishing, Inc. by Capstone Professional
1710 Roe Crest Drive
North Mankato, MN 56003
www.maupinhouse.com

Printed in the United States of America in
Eau Claire, Wisconsin. 008376 072014

Writing, to me, is thinking on paper. This book is dedicated to all the teachers of the world who are never quite satisfied with the status quo. They seek to stretch their students' minds and extend their personal beliefs and ideas as they develop into well-informed, capable problem solvers of tomorrow.

Table of Contents

WHY WRITE? A CASE FOR RAWAC

Now that the Common Core State Standards (CCSS) have refocused attention on reading and writing in all subject areas, social studies teachers are now writing teachers, too.

"The Standards insist that instruction in reading, writing, speaking, listening, and language be shared responsibly within the school. The K-5 standards include expectations for reading, writing, speaking, and listening and language applicable to a range of subjects, including but not limited to ELA. The grades 6-12 standards are divided into two sections, one for ELA and the other for history/social studies, science, and technical subjects. This division reflects the unique, time-honored place of ELA teachers in developing students' literacy skills while at the same time recognizing that teachers in other areas must have a role in this development as well."

-Introduction, Common Core State Standards for English Language Arts & Literacy in History/Social Studies, Science, and Technical Subjects

For the past decade, research has consistently emphasized the need for accomplished writers in the work force. The National Commission on Writing (2003) contends that the "quality of writing [in classrooms] must improve if students are to succeed in college and in life" (p. 7). In a survey of 120 major American corporations, the Commission (2004) discovered that "writing is a ticket to professional opportunity" (p. 3). The business community identified writing as a "threshold skill" for employees, and it voiced dissatisfactions with the writing competency of college-bound students.

In his research, education expert Tony Wagner (2008) found that business leaders complain more about young employees' "fuzzy thinking" and "lack of writing with a real *voice*" than about poor grammar, punctuation, or spelling. Yet, English classes often address the latter more often than the former. It's not that students cannot write, but that they cannot write well.

The National Assessment of Educational Progress (NAEP) concludes that few students can produce precise, engaging, and coherent papers. According to 1998 National Writing Achievement scores, although a majority of students (seventy-eight to eighty-four percent of fourth, eighth, and twelfth graders) have at or above basic writing skills, no more than twenty-seven percent of them are at or above proficient. Only one percent is advanced.

The National Commission on Writing in America's Schools and Colleges (2003) proclaims that a writing revolution will "put language and communication in their proper place in the classroom" (p. 3). They recommend creating a writing agenda for the nation. This includes, but is not limited to the following.

1. doubling the amount of time students spend writing

2. writing across the curriculum

3. assigning out-of-school time for written assignments

The bottom line: Employers expect their employees to provide written and oral reports that are accurate, clear, focused, grammatically correct, and appropriate to format and audience. Our students will be spending time writing informational writing, such as technical summaries and research reports connected to their line of work. Their future projects directly relate to how well they can interpret and communicate knowledge they are learning right now in their subject-area classes. Law students reflect on history and government. Aerospace engineers use math and science. Software designers use technical language.

Since the writing our students will engage in as adults is related to specific content, they need practice learning how to write within their current subject areas. This skill will serve them well later.

The strategies in this resource show teachers how to use writing as a way to learn a subject area, as well as a way to demonstrate that learning. Writing, embedded within social studies classrooms throughout the learning process, will provide students with the practice they need to perform well in their jobs later. The strategies in this book provide content area teachers with several ready-to-go, easy-to-implement strategies that can be used as part of any everyday instruction in their social studies classrooms.

Writing is a skill best acquired through practice. The more often teachers have students write for myriad purposes, the more tools students have in their repertoire for learning. Content-area teachers do not need to *teach* students to write, per se. That is the job of the English Language Arts (ELA) teacher. However, content-area teachers can show students how to write as means to learn the more challenging content they will encounter as they move through the grades.

Of course, there is already some writing incorporated into social studies classes now, for example, socials studies journals or reports. But writing in the social sciences could be so much more valuable to students were we to show them how to use writing to develop ideas, thoughts, and perspectives about a topic in their content areas of study. With just a little effort and time, students can be taught to use writing to process and extend their thinking. They can personalize knowledge, information, and skills by using writing as a way to make connections between social studies and their own lives.

Social studies instruction could be so much richer were students empowered to use writing as a means to learn, rather than as an end in itself. It's time for writing to break free of its lonely fifty-, forty-, thirty-, or twenty-minute scheduled block and be put to use helping students learn social studies.

WRITING IN THE SOCIAL STUDIES CLASSROOM

The ultimate goal of any social studies class is to have students communicate their thinking, rationale, or understanding of subject matter. To communicate learning, you may already engage your students with myriad writing opportunities, and not even realize it. This list is just a sampling of activities in which your students may write as a natural part of their everyday social studies instruction.

WRITING IN SOCIAL STUDIES ACTIVITIES	
brainstorming	classifying
listing	comparing
webbing	describing
predicting	explaining
recording	summarizing
analyzing	note-taking
outlining	justifying

Writing helps students to become proficient with the concepts, skills, and topics in any social studies discipline. They can use writing to help clarify their ideas, record their thinking, internalize their learning, respond to learning, share their ideas, and gain thoughtful feedback to reflect on and adjust their ideas. Writing is a very personal act. Allowing students to engage in writing activities *daily* can only serve to strengthen their understanding of what can often be challenging and sometimes confusing content. And it need not take additional instructional time if it is considered an integral part of an everyday routine. It's that important.

If you are like most social studies teachers, you don't consider yourself a writing teacher. That's fine. No one will be asking you to publish articles in or guarantee your students are ready to write for professional journals. But remember that writing is a valuable learning tool, and it can be used quite effectively—and easily—to help students learn course content. Any topic can incorporate writing to support students as they research, review, and analyze facts, figures, and sources; create timelines; and keep personal notes to help them achieve this end.

INCLUDE WRITING AS A PART OF YOUR INSTRUCTIONAL PLAN

Here are some basics to accomplish integrating writing into your classroom day.

1. **Commit to incorporating writing *every day*.** Hopefully you will see that writing in social studies is not complex or daunting. It can be, if an assignment includes multiple steps or outside research and composition. However, writing

in social studies can also be as simple as completing a concept map (see **Chapter 4**, strategy 2), or summarizing information on a sticky note to post on a class chart (see **Figure 4.9** on page 49). Regardless of the simplicity or complexity of the task, commit to writing in social studies every day.

2. **Provide models of writing in social studies.** Students accept their responsibilities better when they see the value and importance of their work as demonstrated by others. Read social studies-related articles from student-centered journals and magazines such as *National Geographic for Kids* or *History Channel for the Classroom*. Even your local newspaper may have a special write-up about a social studies-related topic now and again. Certainly, every community has current events, or government- or geography-related news to share with interested citizens. Use these resources to enhance your instruction. (Be sure to follow up each reading selection with a writing activity. See **Chapter 4**.)

3. **Make sure every student keeps a social studies notebook.** This can be a three-ring notebook, composition notebook, folder, or unique "foldable" for a particular unit of study. **Chapter 1** addresses how to incorporate journal writing into your social studies routine.

4. **Allow students to listen to and respond to each other's work.** Some written work, such as personal reflections and opinions, is completed for the sake of the person writing. Other writing, however, such as research and reporting, is meant to be shared. Students can sometimes be their own best teachers. Build a collaborative classroom community by allowing students to periodically share their written ideas with the class. Allow students' perceptions and ideas to be used as sounding boards for small group or class discussion or debate. This empowers students to be responsible for their own thinking, and they see that their written ideas are valued and appreciated. Many of the directions for each strategy in this book suggest paired or small group collaboration to complete a writing task, or they suggest providing time for students to share their work.

5. **Keep and maintain a social studies word wall or class learning wall.** Posting related social studies terms is okay. But building students' working vocabulary by displaying terms, definitions, examples, non-examples, and illustrations is better. Another option is to reserve classroom wall space for evidence of students' learning. This can be accomplished by posting written work, diagrams, models, and illustrations of concepts the students have created. Whatever your students write, get it up where they can see it.

INSTRUCTIONAL BASICS FOR INTEGRATING WRITING

Once you have established the overall instructional climate, consider how to incorporate the following objectives for writing.

1. **Set a purpose for the written task.** Know why you are having students do what they are doing. Be sure students know why they are doing what they are doing. If it is just busy work, such as copying words and definitions, copying your notes, or writing down what you tell them to write, the purpose can only be assumed as "to study for the test." These are very un-engaging tasks, and they do not promote "writing." Instead, use writing to develop students' critical thinking skills, help them elaborate on known ideas, and generate individual definitions and summaries that make sense to them. It's their learning. Writing is a tool which allows them to own their learning.

2. **Make time.** Know how much time you want to devote to each activity. If nothing else, stop class five minutes early to allow students to write or respond in their social studies journals. Don't think of this as lost instructional time; think of this as gained learning time.

3. **Set clear expectations.** Be sure students know what will happen to each writing task before they put pencil to paper. Perhaps what they write today will open the class discussion tomorrow.

4. **Model for and monitor students.** When students write in their social studies notebooks, you write in your social studies notebook. When students are writing to contribute to the class, first do one class example. Then, walk the room. Let students know this is an important assignment.

5. **What if students can't or won't write?** Writing in social studies is an opportunity to organize ideas and summarize learning. Don't battle students' refusals. Instead, encourage and support students as needed. Most of the suggestions are not lengthy writing tasks. Help students realize that a little time spent writing will help them learn important concepts.

Oftentimes, struggling readers are also struggling writers. For English language learners (ELLs), writing can be the last communication tool that they master (the others being reading, speaking, and listening). Each strategy in this book offers suggestions for scaffolding writing or differentiating learning to help ELL and at-risk students benefit from writing in social studies, regardless of their writing skill level.

HOW THIS BOOK CAN HELP

Strategies for Writing in the Social Studies Classroom focuses on how you can use writing to develop critical thinking skills and help develop a deeper understand of concepts during all stages of instruction. This book does not go into exhaustive detail about how to teach writing skills, such as organizing content, grammar and punctuation, or the use of specific writing skills like using transition words. It also does not review the key steps to the writing process, nor does it expect social studies teachers to follow them exclusively when assigning essays or position papers. Students already will be learning and practicing all those writing skills within the writing process as part of a comprehensive study in language arts.

Instead, this book capitalizes on the application of writing skills to help students organize the jumble of ideas they likely encounter in a unit of study. For example, when writing a position paper to explain whether they think all citizens should give back to their community, students should be expected to use the writing skills they learned in language arts to compose a thoughtful, meaningful, and coherent essay in class. These expectations would be evident in the evaluation criteria you use when assessing student work. (See **Chapter 8**) In addition, students can use cloze activities, word sorts, and graphic organizers to apply understanding of content-specific vocabulary, record summaries and personal thoughts in notebooks, and organize and respond to informational text, all through the use of writing.

These simple, engaging, and higher-order strategies help you integrate writing during all stages of any instructional model. Most of us learned to write lesson plans following the Madeline Hunter model (1982). This model has undergone several revisions over the years, and we may call different steps by different names. However, it fundamentally remains the same, as seen in **Table 1**. Essentially, any good lesson plan follows this series of steps:

1. Sparking student interest in a topic;

2. Building background and schema before engaging in learning;

3. Using text and multimedia resources to guide learning;

4. Allowing students to apply their learning; and

5. Allowing students to demonstrate mastery of the topic.

Description Of Today's Lesson Plan	Madeline Hunter Lesson Plan Model
Peaks students' interest; gets students personally involved; assesses prior knowledge	Objectives Standards Anticipatory Set
Gets students involved in learning; allows students to build their own understanding; in social studies, discussion, simulation, or activity	Input
Allows students to communicate what they have learned so far; in social studies, text or multimedia information	Modeling Checking for Understanding Guided Practice
Apply acquired knowledge and understandings to new situations; in social studies, unique situations where students may practice their new skill	Guided Practice Closure
Demonstration of student learning	Independent Practice

Table 1: CONTEMPORARY INSTRUCTIONAL MODEL ALIGNED WITH THE HUNTER LESSON PLAN

All the stages of lesson plan development lend themselves to the use of integrated writing activities. Most of the ideas in this book are effective writing strategies—tasks students can utilize during the process of learning in any situation to help them think about, reflect upon, organize, and comprehend any topic in any subject. This book organizes these writing strategies following the Hunter model, starting with ideas to use to engage students in learning and culminating with ideas to use to evaluate or assess student learning. Most strategies follow a similar format:

1. Title
2. Integrated ELA standards
3. Description or summary of the strategy
4. Teacher directions
5. Explanation as to how to use the student activity page, if applicable
6. Differentiation strategies for ELL, at-risk, and accelerated students
7. Suggestions for integrating technology

Many of the strategies include student examples. These are intended to help you visualize what completed student work might look like. Additionally, they may serve as models for students to follow so that you may set clear expectations regarding their notes and summaries.

Writing Strategies in the Social Studies Classroom gives you solid strategies to use at every stage of instruction. You can use writing before students even begin learning about a new concept (see **Chapter 2**). They will be able to use writing all throughout the learning process (see **Chapters 3** through **5**) and write to apply their learning in unique situations (see **Chapter 6**). Additionally, you can evaluate student progress through a unit of study, using both formative and summative writing strategies (see **Chapters 7** and **8**).

Some of the strategies in this resource require just a few minutes; others may be better achieved over several minutes, during one whole class period, or as an outside assignment. Regardless of your comfort level with writing, the step-by-step directions, student examples, and differentiation ideas will be all you need to start students writing in social studies TODAY!

CORRELATIONS TO COMMON CORE ENGLISH LANGUAGE ARTS STANDARDS*

At the elementary level, the Common Core English Language Arts Standards set requirements for reading literature, reading informational text, foundational skills of reading (print concepts at kindergarten and first grade; phonological awareness, phonics and word recognition, and fluency at kindergarten through fifth grades), writing, speaking and listening, and language.

The intermediate-level standards (grades six to twelve) include standards for reading literature, reading informational text, writing, speaking and listening, and language. The suggestions in this book mainly target the Common Core writing standards for grades four through eight, as illustrated in **Table 2** below.

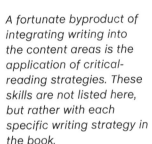

TEACHER TIP

A fortunate byproduct of integrating writing into the content areas is the application of critical-reading strategies. These skills are not listed here, but rather with each specific writing strategy in the book.

STRATEGY	CHAPTER(S)	STANDARDS
Notes and Note-taking	Chapter 1 Chapter 4 Chapter 5	Write opinions or arguments on topics or texts to support claims with clear reasons and relevant evidence.
		Write informational/explanatory texts to examine a topic and convey ideas, concepts, and information through relevant content.
		Draw evidence from informational texts to support analysis, reflection, and research.
		Summarize or paraphrase information in notes and finished work.
		Integrate information presented in different media or formats as well as in words to develop a coherent understanding of a topic or issue.
		Write routinely over time for a range of discipline-specific topics.

Table 2: A CORRELATION OF THE WRITING STRATEGIES IN THIS BOOK TO THE COMMON CORE STATE STANDARDS (CCSS)

STRATEGY	CHAPTER(S)	STANDARDS
Graphic Organizers	Chapter 1 Chapter 4	Determine the main idea(s) and key details of a text. Describe the relationship between scientific ideas or concepts, using language that pertains to time, sequence, and cause/effect. Determine the meanings of words and phrases in text. Identify real-world connections between words and their uses. Write routinely over time for a range of discipline-specific topics.
Personal Reflections	Chapter 2 Chapter 5 Chapter 6	Write opinion pieces on topics or texts, supporting a point of view with clear reasons and relevant evidence. Recall relevant information from experiences; take notes on sources and sort evidence into provided categories. Distinguish their own point of view from that of the author of a text. Write arguments to support claims with clear reasons and relevant evidence. Write routinely over time for a range of discipline-specific topics.
Previewing Text and Making Predictions	Chapter 2 Chapter 3	Recall relevant information from experiences; take notes on sources and sort evidence into provided categories. Use text features and search tools to locate information relevant to a given topic efficiently. Use information gained from illustrations and the words in a text to demonstrate understanding of the text. Analyze how a particular sentence, paragraph, chapter, or section contributes to the development of ideas. Use context as a clue to the meaning of a word or phrase. Use reference materials to determine or clarify the precise meaning of key words and phrases. Write routinely over time for a range of discipline-specific topics.

Table 2 cont.: A CORRELATION OF THE WRITING STRATEGIES IN THIS BOOK TO THE COMMON CORE STATE STANDARDS (CCSS)

STRATEGY	CHAPTER(S)	STANDARDS
Analyzing and Comprehending Text and Sources	Chapter 3 Chapter 5	Write informational/explanatory texts to examine a topic and convey ideas, concepts, and information through relevant content. Conduct research to answer a question. Determine the meanings of words and phrases in text. Identify real-world connections between words and their uses. Use precise, domain-specific vocabulary to inform or explain. Use context as a clue to the meaning of a word or phrase. Determine the meanings of words and phrases in text. Identify real-world connections between words and their uses. Use precise, domain-specific vocabulary to inform or explain. Recall relevant information from experiences; take notes on sources and sort evidence into provided categories. Integrate information presented in different media or formats as well as in words to develop a coherent understanding of a topic or issue. Summarize or paraphrase information in notes and finished work. Integrate information presented in different media or formats as well as in words to develop a coherent understanding of a topic or issue. Write routinely over time for a range of discipline-specific topics.
Summarizing	Chapter 4 Chapter 7	Determine the main idea(s) and key details of a text. Summarize or paraphrase information in notes and finished work. Use precise, domain-specific vocabulary to inform or explain. Ask and answer questions to demonstrate understanding of a text. Describe the relationship between ideas or concepts, using language that pertains to time, sequence, and cause/effect. Describe the logical connection between particular sentences and paragraphs in a text. Compare and contrast the most important points and key details presented in two texts on the same topic. Write routinely over time for a range of discipline-specific topics.

Table 2 cont.: A CORRELATION OF THE WRITING STRATEGIES IN THIS BOOK TO THE COMMON CORE STATE STANDARDS (CCSS)

STRATEGY	CHAPTER(S)	STANDARDS
Research, Simulations, and Independent Projects	Chapter 6	Write opinions or arguments on topics or texts to support claims with clear reasons and relevant evidence.
		Write informational/explanatory texts to examine a topic and convey ideas, concepts, and information through relevant content.
		Write narratives to develop real or imagined experiences or events using effective technique, descriptive details, and well-structured event sequences.
		Integrate information presented in different media or formats as well as in words to develop a coherent understanding of a topic or issue.
		Conduct research projects to answer a question, drawing on several sources and generating additional, related, focused questions for further research and investigation.
		Write informative or explanatory texts, including the narration of historical events.
		Summarize or paraphrase information in notes and finished work.
		Use precise, domain-specific vocabulary to inform or explain.
		Ask and answer questions to demonstrate understanding of a text.
		Produce writing appropriate to task, purpose, and audience.
		Write routinely over time for a range of discipline-specific topics.

Table 2 cont.: A CORRELATION OF THE WRITING STRATEGIES IN THIS BOOK TO THE COMMON CORE STATE STANDARDS (CCSS)

*These Common Core English Language Arts (ELA) Standards have been simplified to span a wider range of grade levels. For specific grade-level standards related to *Reading: Informational Text, Writing,* and *Language,* visit **www.corestandards.org/the-standards/english-language-arts-standards**.

CORRELATIONS TO COMMON CORE ENGLISH LANGUAGE ARTS STANDARDS FOR INTEGRATED TECHNOLOGY

Many of the strategies in this book include suggestions for integrating technology. This particular standard is listed in the Common Core ELA standards. It applies to many of the added technology suggestions, including these listed in Table 3.

APPLICATION	PAGE	STANDARD
Blog	9	Use technology to produce and publish writing as well as to interact and collaborate with others.
Podcast	13	
Twitter	29	
Wiki	19	
Online Research	69	

Table 3: INTEGRATED TECHNOLOGY ACTIVITIES AND THEIR CORRELATION TO COMMON CORE ELA STANDARDS

COMMON CORE WRITING STANDARDS FOR LITERACY IN SOCIAL STUDIES AND TECHNICAL SUBJECTS

Finally, the Common Core Standards include Reading and Writing Standards for Literacy in Social Studies and Technical Subjects for grades six through twelve. Table 4 shows the Common Core Writing Standards for Literacy in Social Studies and Technical Subjects for grades six through eight. Note their parallel nature to the ELA standards listed for specific activities in this book on the previous pages.

STANDARD NUMBER	STANDARD
1	Write arguments focused on discipline-specific content.
2	Write informative/explanatory texts, including the narration of historical events, scientific procedures/experiments, or technical processes.
3	Not applicable.
4	Produce clear and coherent writing in which the development, organization, and style are appropriate to task, purpose, and audience.
5	With some guidance and support from peers and adults, develop and strengthen writing as needed by planning, revising, editing, rewriting, or trying a new approach, focusing on how well purpose and audience have been addressed.
6	Use technology, including the Internet, to produce and publish writing and present the relationships between information and ideas clearly and efficiently.
7	Conduct short research projects to answer a question (including a self-generated question), drawing on several sources and generating additional related, focused questions that allow for multiple avenues of exploration.
8	Gather relevant information from multiple print and digital sources, using search terms effectively; assess the credibility and accuracy of each source; and quote or paraphrase the data and conclusions of others while avoiding plagiarism and following a standard format for citation.
9	Draw evidence from informational texts to support analysis reflection, and research.
10	Write routinely over extended timeframes (time for reflection and revision) and shorter timeframes (a single sitting or a day or two) for a range of discipline-specific tasks, purposes, and audiences.

Table 4: COMMON CORE STATE STANDARDS (CCSS), READING AND WRITING STANDARDS FOR LITERACY IN SOCIAL STUDIES AND TECHNICAL SUBJECTS, GRADES SIX THROUGH TWELVE

CHAPTER ONE

Note-taking in Social Studies

Students do not come to social studies class with an innate instinct for how to take notes. As much as all teachers would like this to be true, it just is not. Note-taking is a learned behavior. Research regarding note-taking (Marzano, 2001) indicates that notes *should* be a work in progress, *should* be used as study guides for tests, *should* be taken frequently, and *should not* be recorded verbatim or copied. Social studies teachers can help develop students' abilities to take notes in class by utilizing one or more of the strategies described in this chapter: maintaining notebooks, creating concept folders, or allowing students to record information using graphic organizers.

Strategy 1: Social Studies Notebooks

Writers' notebooks are a safe place for writers to grow ideas for the writing craft. Social studies notebooks can be a parallel form of these, a continuous record written by students for themselves housing thoughts, ideas, and information before, during, and after learning. They have many benefits for students, including:

- Students can record their thoughts as they think like well-informed and productive citizens.

- Students can record personal ideas related to concepts.

- Students can record ideas to reflect on at a future date.

- Students can communicate using content-specific vocabulary.

- Students can strengthen their overall language and communication skills.

- Students can use the information they recorded to reflect on previous learning and refine and strengthen current understandings.

- Students can save paper, as they can record ideas in one location versus on a variety of teacher-created handouts.

- Students can use them as models in other disciplines, strengthening their overall study skills.

Social studies notebooks do not need to be fancy foldable projects or costly investments. Instead, spiral-bound notebooks or composition books work just fine. Teachers can bring more meaning to their importance by allowing students to personalize their notebooks in some way (related to social studies, of course). Then, as students begin a new unit (see **Chapter 2**), read and learn about a particular concept or topic (see **Chapters 3, 4**, and **5**), extend their knowledge (see **Chapter 6**), and demonstrate their understanding (see **Chapter 7**), their notebooks provide a safe, personal, and meaningful place to record ideas and information, refine their understandings, and reflect on their learning. By the end of a unit of study, students will have a cohesive, complete, and meaningful compilation of their learning, demonstrating their deep understanding of the content.

The following tips will help students learn the value of maintaining their social studies notebooks. Likewise, teachers can use students' notes as a record of learning before, during, and after a unit of study.

1. **Keep the notebook close by.** One never knows when the mood to record information will strike. Writers are encouraged to keep their notebooks handy. Social studies students should keep their social studies notebooks accessible, too. For example, during an election year, students will likely have many opportunities to read about and listen to information related to the candidates, hot topics, and people's perceptions and opinions. Having their notebooks at arms' length would allow students to instantly record what they read or hear about. Then, when the time is right, they can refer to their notes and contribute more meaningfully to class discussions related to the election. If the notebook is not at the ready, learners may miss recording their thoughts, which in turn will lose their personal connection to the content.

2. **Talk about it first.** The act of talking is always easier than the act of writing. Adults and students alike oftentimes will turn to someone close by to discuss their ideas verbally before committing them to print. This is an effective strategy for ELLs and at-risk learners, too. Allow a little chat time before encouraging students to put pencil to paper.

3. **Allow students freedom of thought.** Copying from the board does not constitute note-taking. Introduce and teach ideas through exploration, video, dialogue, debate, print, or any number of instructional strategies. Then, allow students to use their social studies notebooks to record their own thinking. The section in this chapter on the use of graphic organizers is one way to allow students to do this. Additionally, students can use thinking stems (McGregor, 2007) to record their own ideas related to any social studies concept or topic. Thinking stems are simply initial subject/predicate phrases that we use when reflecting upon our experiences or thoughts. They allow us to make personal connections to text, events, and information, making learning more meaningful (and memorable). (See **Figure 1.1.**)

SAMPLE THINKING STEMS

I wonder... I see... I notice... I learned... I remember...
I know that __________, *so* __________.

Figure 1.1: Sample thinking stems

4. **Make time to write every day.** Every day?! Yes, every day. Good writers write every day. To become well-informed and productive citizens, students must internalize their thinking by making notes about the social studies content. Even a five-minute commitment at the end of class is satisfactory for students to think about what they learned and record their ideas in their notebooks. Remember, notebooks are just one strategy for helping students learn the social studies content. If notebooks are not your forte, try the idea of concept folders (below), or use any one of several strategies throughout each stage of the lessons. In order for writing to be an effective strategy to help students learn in social studies, they must have ready access to their notes. A notebook is a convenient place to house information to support students as they learn through writing.

Food for Thought

Will you grade student notes? Before making this decision, weigh the cost-benefit. On one hand, students who do not typically do well on tests can use their participation through writing to help improve their grades. On the other hand, a notebook is evidence of the *process* of learning, not the learning outcome per se. Some would argue that teachers are unfair to grade students as they practice learning. Involve your students in this decision. Decide ahead of time, as a class, whether this work will contribute toward their grade and by how much: Ten percent? Fifty percent? And, what does that look like? Is a complete notebook worth one hundred points and a partial notebook worth fifty points? The evaluation ideas in **Chapter 7** may help you organize these ideas and help you and your students reach a suitable, equitable agreement regarding their written work and its role in their overall grade.

Strategy 2: Concept Folders

Concept folders are mini-notebooks. They can take the form of any foldable format. Foldables are folded and/or cut paper or paper products (such as paper bags) that allow students to organize information in a variety of formats. They may be created to have flaps, mini-pages, or hidden compartments, or they may be one or two sheets of paper folded to make several smaller pages which students can use to take notes. Some foldables are quite elaborate while others have a very simple design. Concept folders might also simply be a three-pronged pocket folder. Regardless of their shape or size, these carry-alls provide students with a place to store all their social studies work (labs, notes, vocabulary, etc.) in one convenient location for the duration of an entire unit of study. For example, if students are learning about the three branches of government, they could create a foldable or pocket folder just for this unit. Then, as they conduct activities, investigations, and simulations; read and write about their personal connections to each branch of government; and summarize their learning, the students have a compilation of their work all in one place. At the end of the unit, students can remove all their work to take home, you can store some or all of it as portfolio evidence, or students can keep everything together for this unit and create a new folder for the next unit.

Concept folders should have all the same components as a social studies notebook, including blank or lined paper for students to record original and personal thoughts and ideas. The difference is notebooks only have room to write. Additional information, such as student activity pages and vocabulary cards, must be stuffed inside the notebook pages or somehow stapled in. With concept folders, if students complete a lab sheet, a copy of this could be stored in one of the pockets. If the students keep their vocabulary words on note cards (for studying purposes), they could keep these in another pocket. Every piece of written work related to a particular topic should have its place in the foldable or pocket folder.

What It Looks Like

Figure 1.2 shows an example of a fourth-grade notebook about Native American tribes of the Southwest. It was made using a brown lunch bag, cut and folded notebook paper, and a rubber band. These entries were added after learning about each tribe. There are enough pages to include specific vocabulary terms, definitions, and illustrations. Students can use their notes to compare different tribes specific to the Southwest and across North America, write quiz questions for review, and create model villages of each tribe. **Figure 1.3** shows how to assemble this foldable notebook.

Figure 1.2: AN EXAMPLE OF A STUDENT'S "NATIVE AMERICANS OF THE SOUTHWEST" FOLDABLE JOURNAL

To make a lunch bag foldable, cut regular notebook paper in half to measure 8 inches by 5¼ inches. Stack several sheets together, then fold them in half (4 inches by 5¼ inches). Insert the fold of the notebook paper into the bottom flap of the lunch bag. Open the pages to the center of the notebook paper. Cut small slits (½ inch or so) down the folds of both the notebook paper and the bag. Place a rubber band around the bag and paper. It should wrap through the center of the notebook paper and fit into the slits. Fold the paper and the bag bottom to lay flat. Fold the top of the lunch bag to cover the notebook paper. Tuck it inside the bottom flap. Voila! Your students have a portable mini-notebook perfect for small note-taking tasks.

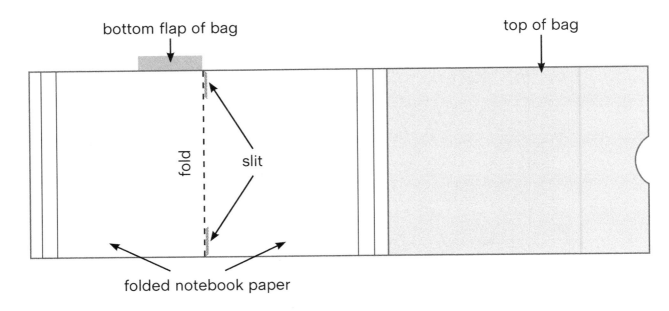

bottom flap of bag

top of bag

fold

slit

folded notebook paper

Figure 1.3: ILLUSTRATION OF THE CONSTRUCTION OF A LUNCH BAG NOTEBOOK

Figure 1.4 shows an example of a social studies notebook for a fifth-grade unit on the Declaration of Independence, the Constitution, and the Bill of Rights. Students kept notes, thoughts, and ideas in the center notebook pages. They stored learning templates, printed informational texts, and vocabulary cards in the pockets. At the end of the unit, students had a complete synopsis of the work they had done and the learning they accomplished. This notebook also provided students with a study guide for the end-of-unit test.

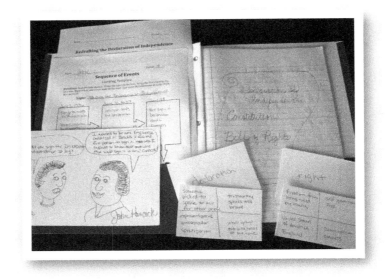

Figure 1.4: AN EXAMPLE OF A COMPLETED POCKET FOLDER SOCIAL STUDIES NOTEBOOK

Figure 1.5 shows a flipbook where students recorded notes about latitude and longitude. As students learned about different lines of latitude and longitude, they listed them at the bottom of each page, then included details and illustrations of each concept.

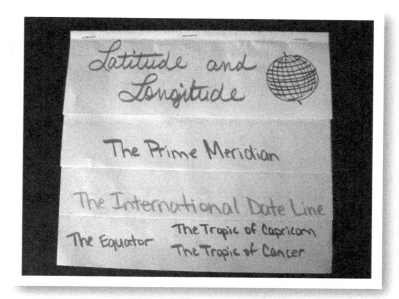
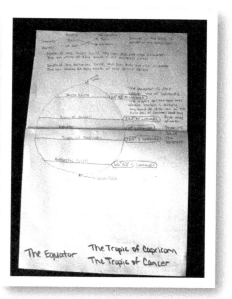

Figure 1.5: FLIPBOOK FOLDABLE NOTEBOOK FOR A UNIT ABOUT LATITUDE AND LONGITUDE

To make a four-page flipbook, fold one sheet of paper along the short side about two inches from the edge. Fold a second piece of paper, also along the short side, about four inches from the edge. Insert the second paper into the fold of the first paper. Staple along the top of the first fold, if desired. Each flap becomes a new page. When students open each flap, they have space to write notes and information and include examples, diagrams, charts, and illustrations.

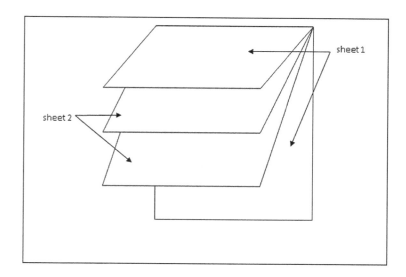

Figure 1.6: ILLUSTRATION OF THE CONSTRUCTION OF A FLIPBOOK

Strategy 3: Graphic Organizers

Graphic organizers for general use are not restricted to reading class. In fact, they are powerful note-taking tools that students can use for any number of learning experiences in any context. They are particularly helpful and useful as students begin to develop an understanding of a multitude of concepts within a specific topic. For example, students learning about cultural diffusion can record details related to this topic using a six-layer main idea wheel (see **Figure 1.7**). A sequencing organizer is perfect any time students need to record a timeline of events or a system or process in government (see **Figure 1.8**). Students can record the causes and effects of events using a cause-and-effect graphic organizer (see **Figure 1.9**). Really, at any point throughout the stages of learning (before, during, and after), students can use pre-printed or student-generated graphic organizers to suit any topic and any comprehension skill. The use of graphic organizers is a highly effective note-taking strategy, so they deserve mentioning here. Graphic organizers are discussed further in **Chapter 4**.

Most graphic organizers are easy to replicate in a social studies notebook. For students who are capable of this task, show them a model or outline illustrating which layout they should use. For students who may have difficulty with this task, provide pre-printed organizers to complete and keep in a pocket folder. If necessary, further differentiate the use of the graphic organizer by completing some of the details, reducing the quantity of work necessary to complete the task.

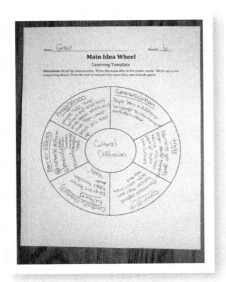

Figures 1.7: MAIN IDEA WHEEL

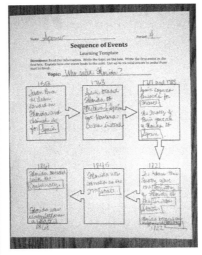

Figure 1.8: SEQUENCING ORGANIZER

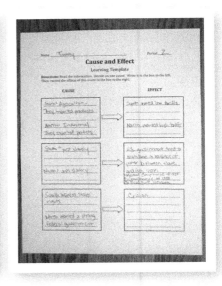

Figure 1.9: CAUSE-AND-EFFECT GRAPHIC ORGANIZER

CHAPTER TWO

Writing to *Engage* Students

The first stage of an effective instructional model in social studies is to engage students with the content. Typically, this is a brief activity designed to get their attention and start them thinking critically (wondering, asking questions). It also generates interest in the upcoming topic. Effective engagement activities include showing a short video, showing a primary source document, posing a thoughtful question, or showing a picture to generate conversation, to name a few. Regardless of the initial activity, the writing strategies in this chapter will provide the needed follow-up by allowing students to record their initial ideas, impressions, and opinions regarding the upcoming unit.

Strategy 1: Opinion Statements

Integrated English Language Arts Skills: Activating Prior Knowledge; Text-to-World Connections; Persuasion; Point of View

Description: One way to grab students' attention when starting a new unit of study is to pose a philosophical question about a current event, a question which requires students to pull from their personal knowledge and analyze their own opinions.

Directions

1. Enlarge the "Opinion Statements" learning template on page 12 so it is poster-sized. Write a "yes" or "no" question at the top. The question should elicit an opinion from the students, requiring them to establish a position on one side of the issue or the other.

2. Poll the students. Record the outcome.

3. Have students discuss their positions in small groups or as a class.

4. Have students list the pros and cons for each side of the debate, each on its own sticky note. Post each idea to the chart in the proper column.

5. Revisit this chart after the unit of study. Re-poll the class. Discuss whether students changed their position and why.

6. Have students reflect on their opinion in their social studies notebooks.

What It Looks Like

The example in **Figure 2.1** shows what a class initially thought about American voting privileges. This question was posed to gain students' interest of the election process. Other examples of effective questions include:

- Should the United States government support more Native American heritage programs?

- Is modern China a better place to live than ancient China?

- Is credit is a good way to expand personal wealth?

- Should the government control economic competition?

- Should the United States Constitution be revisited?

- Is it every person's responsibility to contribute to his or her community?

- Should cultural landmarks continue to be preserved through federal, state, and local taxes?

- Should work with conservation of natural resources be expanded?

Should the United States government require all its eligible citizens to vote? **5** yes **21** no	
PROS	**CONS**
You would get a more realistic, nation-wide result Wouldn't have to do the census anymore because everyone would be voting Everyone should be equally responsible	Dictatorship! What would be the consequences, and who would enforce them? The lines at the polls would be too long People might not make decisions based on the candidates and the issues Would this encourage cheating? Some people might not care about one candidate or the other Some people just don't want to vote People should have a choice as to whether or not they vote

Figure 2.1: A SAMPLE CHART COMPARING STUDENTS' VIEWPOINTS

Adapting to Student Needs

English Language Learners (ELLs) and at-risk students benefit from being able to discuss their ideas in a small group before sharing ideas with the class. Also, they can write a simple sentence or illustration on their sticky note or have their idea transcribed for them by a peer. Following the conclusion of the poll, accelerated students can conduct research about the question posed, and report back to the class as the unit progresses. This adds students' personal involvement to the information presented and adds to the efficacy of all students' abilities to make informed decisions based on facts and knowledge.

Adding Technology

If you have a blog, include the question students are answering on it. Elicit responses from your colleagues and your students' friends and families. Discuss the "going" consensus and why people may be responding this way. As students learn more about the topic, discuss how the research and information they read supports or refutes either or both sides of the debate.

WHAT'S A BLOG?

A blog is kind of like a place to post public journal entries. Each person adds his or her comments, web links, images, media objects, and/or data to a continuous, chronological list of postings. Everyone has access to view everyone else's ideas. Many blogs turn into debating platforms. People have their opinions, and some are quite happy to share them with the world! A word of caution: some blog platforms restrict access, so not everyone can join in.

FREE BLOGGING WEBSITES

BLOGGER
www.blogger.com

THOUGHTS
www.thoughts.com

TUMBLR
www.tumblr.com

WordPress
www.wordpress.com

Opinion Statements

Learning Template

Question: _____

_____

Yes: _____ No: _____

PROS	CONS

Strategy 2: Think-Pair-Share Using Primary Sources

Integrated English Language Arts Skills: Personal Connections; Predicting; Inference

Description: The think-pair-share strategy can be used for many purposes at various times throughout a lesson. One suggestion is to have students use this brainstorming strategy to observe and attempt to identify a piece of realia, better known in today's classrooms as a primary source. It could be a piece of pottery, a map, a trinket, a tool, or any other physical object related to an upcoming topic that students likely have not yet come into contact with. Once they have had their chance to explore the primary source hands-on, allow them to confer and collaborate with their peers regarding the piece's purpose and write their predictions in their social studies notebooks.

Directions

1. Present a primary source (preferably tangible or electronic, if needed).

2. Ask the question, "What is this, and what was it used for?"

3. Allow students about ten seconds to think to themselves.

4. Have students turn to a partner to share their ideas.

5. Allow a few students to share their ideas as a class.

6. Have students record their individual ideas in their social studies notebooks. They should leave room to record the actual use of the item once it is learned during the lesson.

What It Looks Like

The notebook entry in **Figure 2.2** shows how a student might respond to the question "How did the Timucua use the Yaupon holly?" after they have been shown a physical example of the tree or leaves. During the lesson, students would have learned the actual use of this plant and the role it played in the culture of this particular tribe. This would have been included as a second entry following the lesson.

Journal Entry: "How did the Timucua use the Yaupon holly?"

BEFORE LEARNING	AFTER LEARNING
I think the Timucua used the Yaupon holly to make their dwellings.	The Timucua used the Yaupon holly to make a drink called "The Black Drink." They used this drink to remove spiritual and physical impurities.

Figure 2.2: JOURNAL ENTRY COMPLETED AFTER A THINK-PAIR-SHARE ACTIVITY OF A PRIMARY SOURCE

Adapting to Student Needs

ELLs and at-risk students can include a picture or illustration in their social studies notebooks, along with the question and their prediction.

Accelerated students can locate additional electronic pictures of primary sources related to the topic of study and compile them into one slideshow, labeled with their name and use. Printed slides can be added to a bulletin board showcasing artifacts and other evidence of early cultures or other topics.

Adding Technology

Conduct an Internet search of appropriate and relevant podcasts related to an historical topic of study. Allow students to listen to the podcast and summarize the content in their social studies notebooks or record a personal thought related to the podcast.

WHAT'S A PODCAST?

A podcast is an audio recording that is posted to a website for others to listen to. They can be streamed (run through the web link) or downloaded and saved as audio files onto the computer to listen to at a later date.

Strategy 3: Previewing Text: Ask the Expert

Integrated English Language Arts Skills: Activating Prior Knowledge; Text-to-Self, Text-to-Text, and Text-to-World Connections; Previewing Text

Description: This integrated writing strategy can be used at the start of any new chapter or unit. Students work collaboratively to preview a section of text, including vocabulary, pictures and illustrations with their captions, headings, and side notes. Then, they devise a question to ask an expert from that particular era or situation. They could pose a government question to George Washington or an economics question to Alexander Hamilton. Who knows what question students might pose to Alexander the Great? After the chapter, students respond as if they were that expert and share their ideas in small groups or with the class.

Directions

1. Provide each small group of students its own copy of the "Ask the Expert" learning template on page 17. The teams designate one person as the recorder and another person as the sharer.

2. Have students work collaboratively to preview the text and complete the chart. Be sure students know to ask a relevant question related to the information they predict they will read about. For example, students should not ask Zebulon Pike "What is your favorite flavor of ice cream?" because this information will likely not be covered in their informational reading. A better question might be, "Would you say your expedition was more important than, equally important as, or less important than Lewis and Clark's expedition, and why?" Model appropriate questions for the class, if needed.

3. While students work, walk the room to be sure they are focused on their task. Provide the necessary scaffolding to help students arrive at a suitable question using their text preview information.

4. As a class, have the sharer from each group read the question they wish to pose and say to whom they wish to pose it. Record each group's idea on a sentence strip or chart paper for future reference.

5. After students have learned the content, have the groups reflect upon their question. They should work collaboratively to answer the question from the perspective of the person to whom they posed it.

6. Have students record in their notebooks or on drawing paper a cartoon depiction of them asking this person from history the question and the person from history providing a response.

What It Looks Like

The cartoon in **Figure 2.3** shows how a student might depict himself asking John Hancock about his role in the signing of the Declaration of Independence.

Figure 2.3: CARTOON DEPICTION OF "ASK THE EXPERT"

REUSE IT!

Laminate the student copies of the learning template. Have students use dry-erase markers to record the information and their ideas. Erase them when finished, and recollect them for use when introducing another chapter.

Adapting to Student Needs

Once students have adequate practice previewing text, they may begin to complete their preview charts in their social studies notebooks. Allow students who need more support to complete their organizer with a small group. Other students may need less support and can possibly complete their organizer with a partner. Eventually, students should be able to preview text independently.

Adding Technology

Keep an electronic copy of the learning template in a word-processing program. Project the chart onto an interactive whiteboard. Have each group of students concentrate on one feature of the chapter and share their findings. Record each group's summaries on the electronic file. Use the "save as" feature to save the file with the topic name. Print a copy of the preview summary for each student, then allow them to work independently or in pairs to devise a question. Then, follow Steps 4 through 6 listed on the previous page.

Ask the Expert

Learning Template

Directions: Preview the text you will read. Make notes in the boxes. Then, write a question for one person from this era or period in time.

Chapter Title:_____

TEXT FEATURE	WHAT IT TELLS ME
Headings	List the headings here.
Pictures, Illustrations, Charts, Graphs, and Other Visuals	Explain what they show.
Vocabulary	List terms here.
Other	Describe anything else that shows what you will read about.

One question I have for _____ is

_____

Strategy 4: Key Word Predictions

Integrated English Language Arts Skills: Context Clues; Vocabulary Development; Compare and Contrast

Description: Some social studies concepts are quite challenging to students. For example, students may readily comprehend geography, yet struggle with history or government. This strategy allows students to think ahead about what might be a challenging concept, reflect on the use of a term in context, and begin to assimilate their own definition of the term before learning related concepts and reading about complex details.

Directions

1. Write one essential or key term on the line on the "Key Word Predictions" learning template on page 20. Write one or two sentences from a text source using this word in context, or make up your own sentence(s). The sentence(s) should provide enough information for students to attempt to figure out what the word means.

2. Provide each student with a copy of the completed learning template. Have students independently read and reflect on the key word or phrase and sentence(s). They should then write what they think the word means in the first column.

3. Have students work with a partner to share their definitions with each other. They should write their partner's definition in the second column.

4. As a class, ask three or four students to share their ideas. Use the class ideas to generate a class definition of the word, or use a glossary or dictionary to read the "official" definition. Record this class or text definition on the board for students to copy in the third column on their paper.

5. If desired, have students work with their partner to compare all three definitions: theirs, their partner's, and the class's.

6. While students are reading for information, have them reflect back on their initial ideas about this concept. Allow them to record their final understanding of this concept in their social studies notebooks.

What It Looks Like

Figure 2.4 shows an example of a key word prediction for *citizen*. The sentences do not define the term. Instead, the sentences provide information for students to begin to understand what a citizen is and why it is important to know this. Related terms such as *right*, *responsibility*, *privilege*, and *naturalization* will be easier to understand once students have a clear and comprehensive understanding of *citizen* using this key word prediction strategy.

CITIZEN Local officials urge all *citizens* to be on the lookout for suspicious behavior.		
MY DEFINITION	**MY NEIGHBOR'S DEFINITION**	**CLASS OR GLOSSARY DEFINITION**
Someone who has rights	Someone who lives in a city	An official member of a city, state, or nation
How these definitions compare: I thought citizens were people who have rights, but Sarah thought they lived in cities. My neighbor's definition was closer to the glossary definition. Citizens are people who live and work in a city, state, or country.		

Figure 2.4: SAMPLE KEY WORD PREDICTIONS CHART

Adapting to Student Needs

To support ELL and at-risk students, provide illustrations to supplement text whenever possible. For the example above, you might show students pictures from the newspaper of people engaged in various tasks around the community and ask, "How are these citizens helping their community?" Allow students to verbalize their ideas with you or a peer before committing them to print.

Accelerated students can provide everyday examples of the concept, either in writing or with visuals, to share with the class. Post these examples around the room or on a bulletin board throughout the unit of study. Use the examples as reference points to support and extend learning.

Adding Technology

Create a class wiki for each major concept studied throughout the course of the school year. As students learn new information, they may add it to the wiki page. These pages will provide supplemental text and research support as students continue to build on previous knowledge and extend current knowledge. This is also a meaningful way to publish student work. Assign students on a rotating basis to periodically update the wiki. The students will all have an equal opportunity to apply their writing skills for the benefit of the class.

WHAT'S A WIKI?

*A wiki is a collaboratively constructed website or series of related webpages usually used to share factual information about any number of topics. Anyone can add to, delete from, or edit or revise wikis in any way. Alternatively, wikis can also restrict editing privileges. Ideally, only experts who have undisputed information post updates to the site. But if a wiki is open to everyone, anyone can change the content of the wiki page(s). To start your own wiki, visit Wikispaces at **www.wikispaces.com** or Intodit at **www.intodit.com.***

Key Word Predictions

Learning Template

TERM: _____

SENTENCE: _____
_____

MY DEFINITION	MY PARTNER'S DEFINITION	CLASS OR GLOSSARY DEFINITION

How these definitions compare: _____
_____
_____
_____

CHAPTER THREE

Writing while Learning Content: Developing Vocabulary

After engaging students with the content, students begin reading and learning about various topics to acquire facts, details, and information. Most social studies information comes to students in the form of textbooks, articles, and online informational sites. Just as students do not come to social studies class knowing intrinsically how to take notes, they may not have had adequate practice to date with informational reading to naturally apply essential strategies to comprehend what they have read. We read non-fiction much differently than we read fiction. First of all, we have a different purpose. Rather than reading for pleasure or to relate to life's lessons through story, we read non-fiction to gain knowledge. Everything about non-fiction text is different: the structure of the text, the structure of the sentences, and the vocabulary. They all work in a logical, informative manner to provide the information we seek.

Unfortunately, this type of literature can be boring, dry, and monotonous. Students without a passion to read about social studies or any particular topic within social studies will likely tune out, drift off, or simply not read their assignment. So, although students may have participated in and learned something from the activity prior to this point, knowledge presented will stymie them unless you, the social studies teacher, provide adequate support for students to truly learn from the texts they read. The strategies in this chapter help students stay active readers from the first through the last word and provide notes for reflection after the reading.

One component of reading that can directly impact students' comprehension of informational text is their ability to identify and understand essential vocabulary terms. Students who are reading about ancient Mesopotamian civilizations will not learn much if they do not have at least a beginning understanding of the terms *Nile River*, *Tigris-Euphrates River*, *Yellow River*, *irrigation*, and *civilization* (to name a few). The likelihood of students having encountered these terms in fictional reading prior to their instruction in social studies class is minute. As a social studies teacher, do not assume students come to class simply knowing these words or that they will naturally pick them up through content-area reading. Instead, students stand a much greater chance of learning and comprehending informational text when essential words are taught directly (Marzano, 2001). One strategy for developing vocabulary, *Key Word Predictions*, can be found on page 18 in Chapter 2. The following are four additional strategies to help students gain a working understanding of essential terms they will encounter in text.

Strategy 1: Vocabulary Comparisons

Integrated English Language Arts Skills: Vocabulary Development; Compare and Contrast

Description: This strategy requires students to have a deep and thorough understanding of key terms. This strategy assumes students have had direct instruction with related terms and are ready to apply their understanding in a higher-level context.

Directions

1. Print one copy of the "Vocabulary Comparisons" learning template on page 24 for each student.

2. Read the directions and the example together.

3. If needed, complete one example using a current term as a class.

4. If desired, provide a list of items from which to make comparisons, and insist that students choose from the list.

5. Have students keep a copy of their comparisons in their notebooks.

6. As students become proficient at developing comparisons, encourage them to think of and record their own. Any comparison is acceptable as long as they justify it appropriately.

What It Looks Like

Figure 3.1 shows how a student might make comparisons with terms from a unit on ancient Egyptian cultures.

A Pharaoh is like the post office because he is the ruler of everything within the land, just as a post office rules over the mail.

Pyramids are like filing cabinets because they are very organized, and they hold important things you don't need anymore but can always get to if you want.

Figure 3.1: SAMPLE VOCABULARY COMPARISONS

Adapting to Student Needs

If needed, list the terms for ELL and at-risk students before copying the template. You might also provide a list of common ideas for them to choose from to make their comparisons. Students who cannot write could have their ideas transcribed for them, or they could be allowed to illustrate and label their ideas.

Another differentiation strategy is to pair students for this activity, and have each pair share their ideas with another pair of students (another version of a "pair-share"; see page 13). This increases students' verbal discussion of each term and provides peer support and collaboration for what can be a very challenging assignment.

Accelerated students can explain and illustrate their ideas on note cards. Post select examples on a word wall for students to refer to throughout the unit.

Adding Technology

Have one or two students create a spreadsheet listing each social studies term and all the students' common ideas for each term. Print this page and enlarge it using a poster printer. Post it in the room throughout the duration of the unit.

Alternatively, use an online poster-building website, such as Glogster (**www.edu.glogster.com**), to have students artfully type their comparisons. An example of the two comparisons is shown in **Figure 3.2** using Glogster.

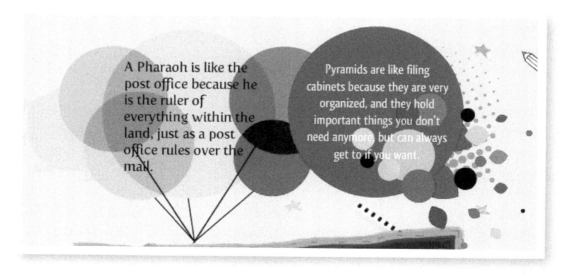

Figure 3.2: VOCABULARY COMPARISONS COMPLETED USING THE GLOGSTER WEBSITE

Vocabulary Comparisons

Learning Template

Directions: Think about the meaning of each term. Compare the term to a common idea. Explain how this term and the idea you listed are *alike*.

Example: *Interest* is like a *lawnmower* because *the grass keeps piling up, just like the money owed to the bank.*

TERM	COMMON IDEA	EXPLANATION

Strategy 2: Mapping Vocabulary Words

Integrated English Language Arts Skills: Vocabulary Development; Compare and Contrast

Description: Vocabulary mapping is a high-yield strategy ("Just Read Now" project) that helps students learn essential terms in social studies or in any other content area. As with concept maps, the essential term takes center stage on the page. Then, students include four related components (a definition, an illustration, an original sentence, and examples/non-examples/characteristics) in each of four areas surrounding the term.

Directions

1. Print one copy of the "Vocabulary Maps" learning template on page 28 for each student. This template provides space for three terms. Make enough copies so that each student has adequate maps for each of his or her social studies terms.

2. Read the directions as a class.

3. If needed, complete one example as a class using a current term.

4. Have students keep a copy of their comparisons in their notebooks.

5. Have students copy this template in their social studies notebooks—one template for each term—to eliminate the use of copies. Another option is to have students copy the template on note cards.

6. Another option is to have students copy the template on note cards and bind them in one corner with a ring clip, yarn, or a rubber band.

7. Students can also make their own vocabulary map templates using folded paper:

8. Fold a sheet of paper twice to make four quadrants.

9. Fold the corner where both folds meet on a slight angle. This will make a triangle.

10. Open the paper. Trace the folds with marker or colored pencils. The triangle fold should make a center square in the center of the page. Have students complete the template as shown on page 28.

What It Looks Like

The vocabulary maps in **Figure 3.3** were completed using folded copy paper. Students can easily make one map for each term to keep in their notebooks. These maps include a definition, an illustration, an example, and an original sentence.

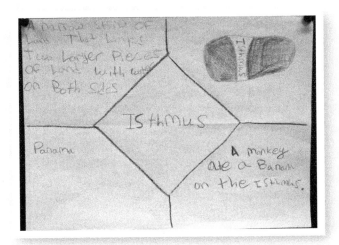 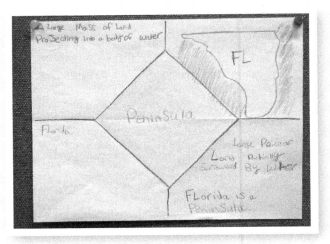

Figure 3.3: STUDENT EXAMPLES OF VOCABULARY MAPS USING FOLDED PAPER

The example in **Figure 3.4** shows how a student might copy and complete the vocabulary map template for terms related to the Declaration of Independence in his or her social studies notebook. If the term is found in the original document, it is quoted on the right side of the page. This example also includes illustrations for each term, another highly effective vocabulary learning strategy (Marzano, 2001).

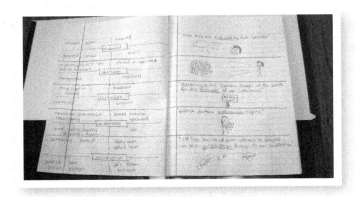

Figure 3.4: STUDENT EXAMPLE OF VOCABULARY MAPS IN A SOCIAL STUDIES NOTEBOOK

Adapting to Student Needs

Allow at-risk and ELL students to work in pairs or small groups to make their vocabulary maps. Listing non-examples can be challenging. Instead of requiring non-examples in the bottom right quadrant, allow students who may benefit to illustrate their terms instead, as in the examples above.

Accelerated students can create quiz cards for each term. Have them write the term on the front of a note card, then create their quadrants on the back. Before administering a vocabulary quiz, have pairs or small groups of students use the cards to quiz each other.

Adding Technology

Create this template using a word-processing program. Use the shapes tools (iWork Pages) or SmartArt (Microsoft Word) functions to design and create your own template for students. Then, this template can be emailed to students for them to complete either at school (if adequate computers are available) or at home.

If you have a Google account, you can create your template online via Google Docs (**www.google.com/google-d-s/tour1.html**) and then invite your students to log on and revise a single document online. Visit Google Apps for Education to learn more: **www.google.com/apps/intl/en/edu/k12.html**.

Vocabulary Maps

Learning Template

Directions: Write each term on the line in the center of the map. Write the definition in the upper left space. Write the characteristics of the term in the upper right space. List examples and non-examples in the lower spaces.

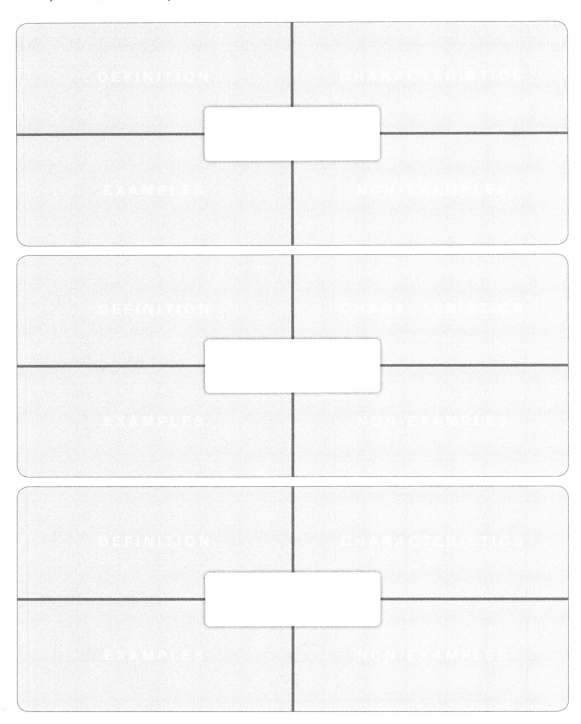

Strategies for Writing in the Social Studies Classroom

Strategy 3: Sentence Summaries

Integrated English Language Arts Skills: Vocabulary Development; Summarizing

Description: This strategy develops students' general language arts skills while simultaneously strengthening their understanding of essential vocabulary terms. Students write one of four different types of sentences (e.g., statement, question, exclamation, and command) using their vocabulary terms. Then, they pass their paper to the student on their right to add an additional sentence using a different term. At the end of four rounds, students have one paper using four terms, each in an original sentence.

Directions

1. Print one copy of the "Sentence Summaries" learning template on page 31 for each student.

2. Read the directions together.

3. Post a list of vocabulary terms to review, or allow students to have access to their social studies notebooks, which include the terms and definitions.

4. Set a short time limit, about thirty to sixty seconds. Have each student write one sentence on the paper. Students do not need to start at the top of the page. They may write any one of the four types of sentences to start using any one of their vocabulary terms.

5. When time is up, have students fold their paper in half. Then, they pass it to the person on their right. Once everyone has a different paper, start the timer again. Students should open their paper and write a second sentence to complete the page using a second vocabulary word. For example, if the person to his or her left wrote a command, the student may write a statement, a question, or an exclamation using a different term than the one previously used. Keep time again, for about thirty to sixty seconds.

6. Continue play for two more rounds, until all the sentences are complete. Then, have students pass the papers to the right once more. The fifth person opens the paper and independently reads all the sentences.

7. Have three or four students each share a statement with the class, three other students share a question, three other students share an exclamation, and three others share a command.

8. Collect the students' papers to use for assessment purposes (see **Chapter 7**).

What It Looks Like

You might see the sentences in **Figure 3.5** included on a paper during a unit about economics.

Statement: My friend was willing to <u>trade</u> his candy for my taffy.

Question: If you want to borrow money, what <u>capital</u> are you willing to put up?

Command: Make your <u>opportunity cost</u> greater by finding the best value for your money.

Exclamation: I can't find any peanut butter-filled choco-chunky cookies because of <u>scarcity</u>!

Figure 3.5: SENTENCE SUMMARY EXAMPLES

Adapting to Student Needs

Provide examples on the board of each type of sentence (see **Figure 3.6**). You may choose to allow students to work in pairs when applying this strategy for the first time in your classroom.

SENTENCE TYPES

Statement:	A declaration that has a subject and predicate, usually in that order, and ends with a period (.)
Question:	An interrogative expression that ends with a question mark (?)
Command:	An expression that gives an order and ends with a period (.) or exclamation point (!)
Exclamation:	A sharp or sudden expression that ends with an exclamation point (!)

Figure 3.6: TYPES OF SENTENCES

Accelerated students can write extended sentences that include phrases, dialogue, hyperbole, onomatopoeia, or any number of creative writing strategies.

Adding Technology

Have one or two students type the sentences in a large font using a word-processing program or on a poster in Glogster (**www.edu.glogster.com**). Print the sentences or posters, then post them on a word wall throughout the unit of study.

Another option is to have students tweet their sentences. You can make a classroom Twitter account (**twitter.com**) and have students submit handwritten tweets (sentence summaries of 140 characters or less) each week. For example: *Make your OPPORTUNITY COST greater by finding the best value for your money. #Command #Economics*

Sentence Summaries

Learning Template

Directions: Choose one word from your vocabulary words. Write one sentence on the lines in one of the boxes using that word. Pass the paper to your right. Look at what your neighbor wrote. Choose a different word. Then write a different type of sentence in another box with this second word. Do this two more times so that you have written four different types of sentences with four different vocabulary words.

STATEMENT

_____

_____

_____

QUESTION

_____

_____

_____

COMMAND

_____

_____

_____

EXCLAMATION

_____

_____

_____

Strategy 4: Vocabulary Word Sort

Integrated English Language Arts Skills: Vocabulary Development; Similarities and Differences

Description: Some social studies topics may have an abundance of related vocabulary terms, perhaps too many for students to learn within the given timeframe of a particular unit. Marzano (2001) contends that, in order for vocabulary learning to be meaningful, students should be required to truly learn between five and seven critical terms and phrases from any particular unit of study. Within the context of teaching social studies, some topics are quite vocabulary-heavy, and students may be encountering these words for the first time.

This strategy encourages repeated exposure to related vocabulary terms, whether you decide to directly instruct the words or allows students to encounter them in context. Students work collaboratively to first sort the words into two, three, or four categories, then write to explain why the words were sorted in this manner.

Directions

1. Write each vocabulary word for a current topic or unit in its own space on the "Vocabulary Word Sort" learning template on page 34.

2. Copy the words so that each pair or small group of students has one copy of the set.

3. Cut the words apart and place them in an envelope or clear zipper bag, or simply clip them together.

4. Have students work collaboratively with their group to discuss the words and sort them according to how they relate to each other. Leave the number of categories open. Students may sort the words into two sets, three sets, or even four sets. Groups may sort words using categories that differ from each other.

5. Have students summarize their sorting strategy in their notebooks. Then, have one person from each group share with the class which words they placed together with justification.

What It Looks Like

Figure 3.7 shows how students sorted words related to a unit about the Constitutional Convention. When questioned as to why they included *privilege* in the "pitfalls" category, one student responded that they themselves (the *privileged*) were an example of a faction.

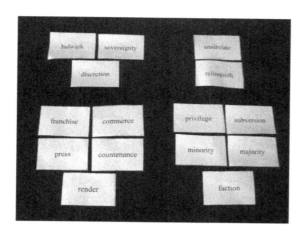

Figure 3.7: EXAMPLE OF SORTED VOCABULARY TERMS FROM A UNIT ABOUT THE CONSTITUTIONAL CONVENTION AND A CORRESPONDING NOTEBOOK ENTRY JUSTIFYING EACH CATEGORY

NOTEBOOK ENTRY

1. Goals: bulwark, sovereignty, discretion. They all have to do with the reason to have a Constitutional Convention.

2. Tools: franchise, commerce, press, countenance, render. They explain how people can get things done.

3. Pitfalls: privilege, minority, faction, subversion, majority. They all have to do with groups that want their arguments included.

4. Get Over It!: annihilate, relinquish. They explain bad ideas that need to be forgotten.

Adapting to Student Needs

Provide at-risk and ELL students with pictures illustrating the vocabulary terms. Encourage collaboration from each group member throughout the sorting process.

Challenge accelerated students to sort and then resort the terms using different categories. Their social studies notebooks will then have two summaries to justify the relationship among the words for each sorting exercise.

Adding Technology

Create a PowerPoint slide listing all the terms, each in its own text box. Project the slide onto an interactive whiteboard, then work as a class to sort the terms into categories. On a second slide, type a summary as a class. Print the slides, and post them on a learning wall throughout the unit of study.

Scribblar (**www.scribblar.com**) is a free interactive whiteboard site.

Vocabulary Word Sort

Learning Template

Directions: Write your vocabulary words, one in each space. Cut the words apart. Sort them into categories. Place words that are related into one category. Place other words that are related into a second category. You may have up to four categories. Summarize how you sorted the words. Use a sheet of paper. Explain why you sorted them this way.

CHAPTER FOUR

Writing while Learning Content: Reading for Information

As discussed in the previous chapter, we read non-fiction with a different purpose than we read fiction. Stephanie Harvey (1998) writes that students (and adults alike) engage in non-fiction text to gain information, learn something new, develop a deeper understanding of prior knowledge, and to... have fun? Yes, non-fiction reading can be fun.

The strategies in **Chapter 1** assume students begin their social studies understanding through activity first. **Chapter 2** delved into how students develop deeper understanding through content-area reading. **Chapter 3** focused on how students can use writing to learn essential vocabulary. This chapter provides writing strategies for students to make personal connections while reading informational text. Oftentimes, this content-area reading comes to students through published textbooks. Teachers, especially those just beginning their careers, want to rely on published texts to provide students with the information they need to be successful with social studies content and on statewide and national assessments.

> "...proficient readers connect what they read to their own lives... this type of reading promotes engagement and enhances understanding."
>
> — Stephanie Harvey, *Nonfiction Matters: Reading, Writing, and Research in Grades 3-8*

In addition to published texts, students can also gain information through articles in social studies-related magazines such as *TIME for Kids*, local or national newspaper articles, non-fiction books, online encyclopedias or other reliable electronic media such as The History Channel Classroom, and a host of additional sources. There is a lot of information to read! Regardless of the text that students read to learn, the writing strategies in this chapter allow students to make personal connections with non-fiction literature to develop their social studies literacy.

Strategy 1: Using Graphic Organizers

Integrated English Language Arts Skills: Predicting; Brainstorming; Webbing; Main Idea and Details; Compare and Contrast; Cause and Effect; Vocabulary Development; Making Inferences; Drawing Conclusions; Fact and Opinion; Sequencing; Note-taking; and Summarizing

Description: The use of graphic organizers was first introduced in **Chapter 1** as an effective note-taking strategy. This section serves as a reminder about their value and importance to help students sort, categorize, and comprehend a multitude of information during non-fiction reading. Additionally, graphic organizers serve as effective reviews of key concepts throughout a unit of study and as valuable study guides leading up to a summative assessment of the content.

Directions

1. First decide which literacy skill(s) the text lends itself to, such as compare and contrast, sequencing, or main idea and details.

2. Provide a graphic organizer to match these skills. For example, if students are reading to find the main idea and related details of a particular text, a web is well suited to this purpose.

Teachers have the option of printing graphic organizers for student use or, after having completed similar organizers, students can copy the templates into their notebooks to complete. Another option is to begin or complete a class organizer to post on a learning wall to reference throughout a unit of study. Regardless of the method, students should be encouraged to record information using graphic organizers to help them sort through and apply meaning to what can otherwise become overwhelming and mundane informational reading.

What It Looks Like

Figures 4.2 and **4.3** show two examples of graphic organizers. The first shows how a student might record facts about three of the seven ancient natural wonders. Additional tree diagrams could be completed so all students have notes on all seven wonders. Or, students could work in small groups to share information they learned on the three they studied while their partners record facts about the wonders they did not study in their notebooks. The second organizer shows how a student might use a triple Venn diagram to compare the economies of ancient Rome, Greece, and Egypt. Three other examples of graphic organizers may be found on page 8 (Figures 1.7, 1.8, and 1.9).

Adapting to Student Needs

Consider students' abilities when deciding the amount of information expected for each organizer's completion. For example, you may consider providing the main ideas for at-risk and ELL students, requiring them to only read and record the details. Or, you may consider reducing the number of details at-risk and ELL students need to record by providing one and having them record a second. For students who are reading two or more grade levels below their current grade level, you might consider providing them with most of the information and having them read and record just one additional fact.

Accelerated students may require little direction once they have been shown how to complete a graphic organizer, and your expectations for their work may be increased. For example, if most of the class has a graphic organizer for finding and recording six facts, accelerated students might have a graphic organizer for finding and recording eight facts. Or, if most of the class is to find three commonalities between two ideas, accelerated students might be expected to find five.

Adding Technology

Graphic organizers are easily found by conducting an online search. See **Figure 4.1** for a list of electronic and published resources for graphic organizers

ONLINE	BOOKS
Freeology.com **www.freeology.com/graphicorgs**	*A Guide to Graphic Organizers* by James Bellanca
Houghton Mifflin Harcourt (EduPlace) **www.eduplace.com/graphicorganizer**	*The Teacher's Big Book of Graphic Organizers* by Katherine McKnight
EdHelper **www.edhelper.com/teachers/graphic_organizers.htm**	*Great Teaching with Graphic Organizers* by Patti Drapeau

Figure 4.1: RESOURCES FOR GRAPHIC ORGANIZERS

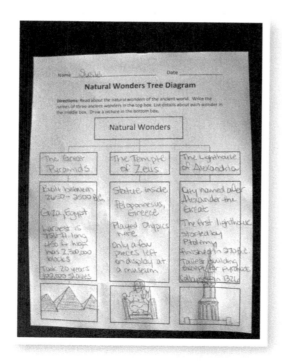

Figure 4.2: AN EXAMPLE OF A TREE DIAGRAM GRAPHIC ORGANIZER

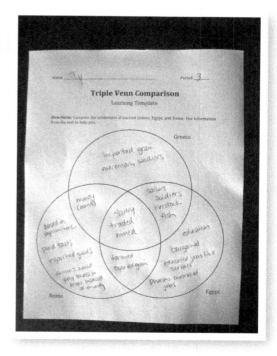

Figure 4.3: AN EXAMPLE OF A TRIPLE VENN DIAGRAM GRAPHIC ORGANIZER COMPARING THE ECONOMIES OF ANCIENT GREECE, ROME, AND EGYPT

Strategy 2: Concept Maps

Integrated English Language Arts Skills: Summarization; Main Idea and Details; Vocabulary Development

Description: An effective prewriting strategy is to create a concept map or web about a particular topic. Generally, the main idea holds center stage in the middle of the web, and related ideas connect to it by a series of spokes. This strategy can be applied in reverse as students read informational text. Their task is to create the web from which this text was generated.

The example in **Figure 4.4** shows a prewriting concept map for the topic of "bullying." This is one way students might plan an essay to explain what it means to bully.

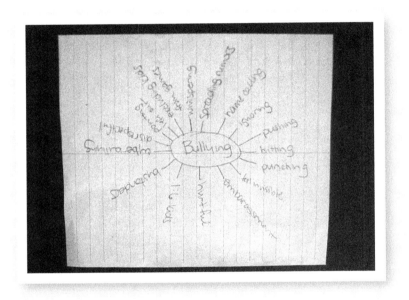

Figure 4.4: EXAMPLE OF STUDENT-GENERATED CONCEPT MAP

Directions

1. Provide a copy of the "Concept Map" learning template for each student or for each pair of students.

2. Read the directions together as a class. Have students read the informational text selection independently, with partners, or in small groups.

3. As a class, decide upon the main concept. Have each student write it in the center, shaded circle.

4. Allow students time to complete their graphic organizer independently, with partners, or in small groups.

5. Review the organizer as a class. Discuss the information students read about. They should summarize the information in one sentence at the bottom of the page.

What It Looks Like

The concept map in **Figure 4.5** shows how a student might have organized ideas presented in an online article explaining civic responsibility.

Figure 4.5: SAMPLE CONCEPT MAP ON THE TOPIC OF CIVIC RESPONSIBILITY

Adapting to Student Needs

For students who need additional scaffolding and support, list the main concept and one or two related ideas in the web before copying it for them. Then, as they read, they find additional related ideas to add to the web. Allow ELL and at-risk students to work with a partner to complete the organizer. Encourage them to discuss the pictures, illustrations, diagrams, and other visuals on the text pages.

Accelerated students can generate questions about the text selection to pose to the class. Post these questions on a chart to use as a review to start the next day's lesson.

Adding Technology

Use application software such as Kidspiration® or Inspiration® to allow students to create an electronic concept map.

For information about this software, visit the Inspiration website, **www.inspiration.com**.

Additionally, Microsoft Word provides a bank of graphic organizers students can insert within a word-processing document. This "Smart Art" includes organizers for lists, processes, sequencing, cycles, and more.

Concept Map

Learning Template

Directions: Think about the informational text you just read. Write the main concept in the center circle. Complete this concept map (or web) to show how ideas from the text relate to the main concept.

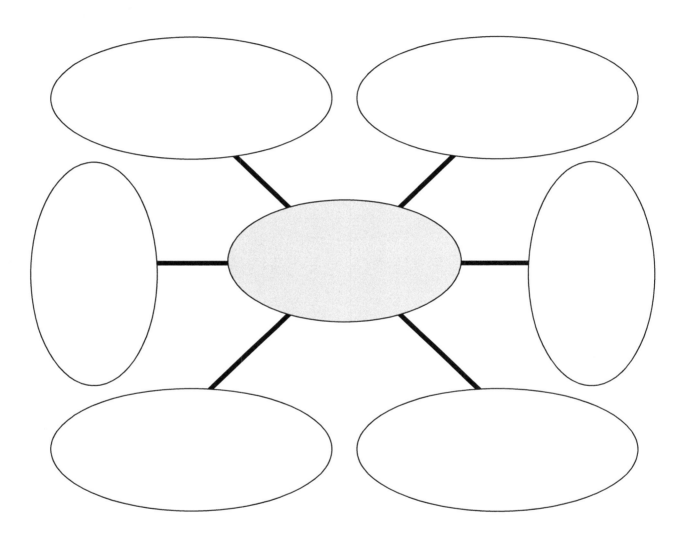

This text was mostly about _____

_____

_____

_____

Strategy 3: Summarizing

Integrated English Language Arts Skills: Summarizing; Main Idea and Details; Vocabulary Development

Description: Summarizing is simply restating the main point in as few words as possible using language that anyone can understand. To be successful summarizers, students must be able to read, interpret, comprehend, analyze, and synthesize information. Then, they organize it in a way that captures the main ideas and supporting details—but in their own words. There are many ways to summarize. The use of main idea and sequencing graphic organizers are particularly helpful for summarizing social studies content. Figure 1.7 shows an example of one such organizer, called a main idea wheel (see page 8).

To help students really grasp the most important ideas, they can summarize a text selection in one paragraph, one sentence, or one word or phrase. These tasks are increasingly more challenging. One might think that writing a paragraph is more complex than writing one word, but to summarize an entire text selection in one word, students must truly have sorted through all the important and non-essential information. The directions that follow explain how to help students attend to the challenging task of summarizing.

Directions

1. Have students read a text selection independently, in pairs, or in small groups.

2. Distribute the "Summarizing" learning template on page 43 to each student. Let students complete it with their reading partners.

3. Model how to identify the main idea and most important examples from a text. Students should copy these down in the chart on the template.

4. Then, have students work collaboratively to identify words that may be confusing or cause the information to seem vague or unclear. For example, students may wish to change *verify* to *prove* or *document* to *paper*. The example in **Figure 4.6** shows how vocabulary in a particular text might be simplified.

5. Model for students how to use the notes they took on the learning template to write a simple summary of the informational text.

6. As a class, see if students can meet either challenge of writing a one-sentence or one-word summary.

7. Provide continued support and scaffolding until students are confident in their abilities to summarize text on their own or with their reading partners.

What It Looks Like

The example in **Figure 4.6** shows how a student might have summarized the online *Time for Kids* article, "A Nation at War." Words that have been simplified include *declare*, *abolished*, and *intact*.

Abraham Lincoln was elected President of the United States in 1860. The southern states seceded, or split, from the rest of the nation. The American Civil War began on April 12, 1861 when shots were fired at Fort Sumter in South Carolina. At first, the war began over states' rights. Abraham Lincoln wanted to keep all the states together. Then, he signed the Emancipation Proclamation on January 1, 1863. This freed slaves in the southern states. Two years later, the northern states won the Civil War. Andrew Johnson announced the end of the war, and Congress signed the 13ᵗʰ Amendment outlawing slavery.

Figure 4.6: EXAMPLE OF SUMMARIZED TEXT WITH SIMPLIFIED VOCABULARY

Adapting to Student Needs

For particularly challenging passages, provide the main idea to ELL and at-risk students. As they read, they should be identifying important details. Also, provide a thesaurus for them to use to modify higher-level words. They might also benefit from illustrating their summary, which may help when they review it later to study for a test.

Have accelerated students research a current event related to an historical event or a topic of study. Allow them time to share their findings with the class. As a class, discuss how the events of the present compare to the events of the past.

Adding Technology

Have students type their summaries in a word-processing program, insert an illustration, and print them. As they continue learning about the topic, they can compile their summaries into one complete collection of historical, geographical, economic, or civic events.

Summarizing

Learning Template

Directions: You can summarize a text selection by finding the main idea and making the information more understandable.

1. Find the main idea and most important details.

WHAT IS THE MAIN IDEA? WRITE IT AS IT APPEARS IN THE TEXT.
WHAT ARE DETAILS THAT SUPPORT THE MAIN IDEA? WRITE ONLY THE MOST IMPORTANT DETAILS.

2. Re-read the main idea and details. Cross out words that are confusing. Replace them with simpler words.

3. Use another sheet of paper. Rewrite your sentences to summarize the information.

Challenge! Try summarizing the information in just one sentence. Then, try summarizing the information in just one word or one phrase.

Strategy 4: SQ3R

Integrated English Language Arts Skills: Predicting; Main Idea and Details; Summarizing; Text Structure

Description: The Survey, Question, Read, Recite, Review (a.k.a., SQ3R) method of note-taking has been around for quite some time. It was originally suggested by Derek Rowntree back in the 1970's. It remains an effective previewing and predicting strategy for students still today. Essentially, students follow the steps in the title to systematically preview, read, and review informational text.

Directions

1. Provide each student with a copy of the "SQ3R" learning template on page 45. Explain that they will follow the steps to survey, question, read, recite, and review information.

2. Discuss which steps students will complete *before* reading (*survey* and *question*). Allow them time to survey the text and write questions they will have answered related to the headings. Students will need to use additional paper.

3. Next, discuss which steps students will complete *during* reading (*read* and *recite*). Allow students time to read the text and answer the questions they wrote.

4. Finally, discuss which step students will complete *after* reading (*review*). Pair students up to review the text at the start of the next class period.

What It Looks Like

The example on page 46 shows how a student might have previewed a text selection related to ancient Mesopotamia.

Adapting to Student Needs

Allow time for at-risk and ELL students to discuss their idea(s) with a partner as they survey, question, read, and recite the text. Also, these students could draw and label the information instead of writing entire sentences to answer the questions.

Have accelerated students summarize their notes using a word-processing or desktop publishing program. Use these summaries as part of a class review. If desired, make a copy to act as additional study notes for all the students.

Adding Technology

Instead of having students ask and answer questions on paper, have students who have the capability tweet or text you the questions and answers. The next day, share the tweets and texts with the class.

WHAT'S A TWEET?

*A tweet is a short message (140 characters or fewer) posted to Twitter, an online microblogging service (**twitter.com**).*

SQ3R

Learning Template

Directions: You are about to read an informational text selection. Use this page to organize your thinking before, during, and after reading.

SURVEY

Title: _____

Summarize the introduction. _____

_____

List all the headings here.

_____   _____

_____   _____

_____   _____

_____   _____

Restate the summary. _____

_____

Read the questions at the end of the text selection.

QUESTION

Use another sheet of paper. Change each of the headings you listed above into a question. Leave room beneath each question to write the answer.

READ

Read the informational text.

RECITE

Answer the questions you wrote in your own words. Also, answer any questions at the end of the chapter.

REVIEW

Review this page and your questions and answers each day.

SQ3R

Student Example

SURVEY

Title: _Geography, History, and Government of Ancient Mesopotamia (http://mesopotamia.mrdonn.org)_

Summarize the introduction.

People lived in ancient Mesopotamia over 6,000 years ago. They made big cities, developed written language, and built huge structures.

List all the headings here.

History	Sumer
Geography	Babylon
Agriculture	Assyria
Trade and Commerce	

Restate the summary.

Ancient Mesopotamia was a great civilization. They did many things like build large cities with huge buildings and develop writing.

Read the questions at the end of the text selection. *There were none.*

QUESTION

History
What major events occurred in ancient Mesopotamia? *The earliest evidence of people is from 5,000 B.C. Many cultures covered many periods through Mesopotamian history. The fall of Nineveh happened in 612 B.C. The fall of Babylon happened in 539 B.C. Alexander the Great conqued Persia in 330 B.C.*

Agriculture
What crops did the ancient Mesopotamians grow? *Mesopotamia means "land between two rivers." Here they had wildlife and vegetation. They planted wheat, barley, dates, and vegetables including cucumbers, onions, apples, and spices. They irrigated their crops because it did not rain much.*

Babylon
What is Babylon, and why is it important? *Babylon was a highly organized ancient civilization that arose after the Sumerians settled Mesopotamia. It was in the south, by the Persian Gulf. Babylon had impressive cities. Its culture was based on law. Its crops flourished, and the most important God was Marduk.*

Strategy 5: Note-taking

Integrated English Language Arts Skills: Main Idea and Details; Sequencing; Text-to-Self, Text-to-World, and Text-to-Text Connections

Description: Students do not typically enter the intermediate grades as expert note takers. Usually, one of two things happens. Either they write down every detail, regardless of importance or meaningfulness, or they write nothing. As a content-area teacher, you have an opportunity to help students develop important and critical note-taking skills. By doing so, you show them how to identify the main ideas and details, organize content into sequential structure, and/or identify how the information is relevant to them through past experiences, current events, or previous learning.

Following are four strategies students can use to practice note-taking skills within the context of their social studies learning.

Notebooks

This book started with an overview of the use of notebooks throughout a unit of study (see **Chapter 1**). One use of notebooks is for students to take notes before, during, and after informational reading. The student template on page 52 is one example that mirrors the two-column note-taking method. With two-column notes, students record the main ideas on the left and their corresponding details on the right. The two-column note-taking method is also useful for vocabulary development. Students list the words on the left and the corresponding definitions on the right. The example in **Figure 4.7** shows a student's two-column notes for vocabulary words related to the Industrial Revolution. Students can fold the words back to quiz themselves using the definitions, or they can fold the definitions back to quiz themselves using the words.

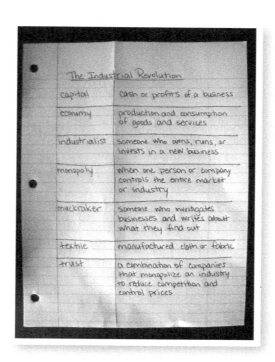

Figure 4.7: EXAMPLE OF TWO-COLUMN NOTES

The three-column note-taking method adds a third column where students list questions in the far left column (they can also cite their resources here if they are reading more than one text), essential information in the center column, and personal reflections in the right column. When using this strategy for vocabulary development, students have a third column to include an original sentence or an illustration. The template on page 53 is useful when showing students this strategy. Once they become familiar with the strategy, they can simply draw a chart in their notebooks to complete. **Figure 4.8** shows a student's three-column notes recorded as a notebook entry.

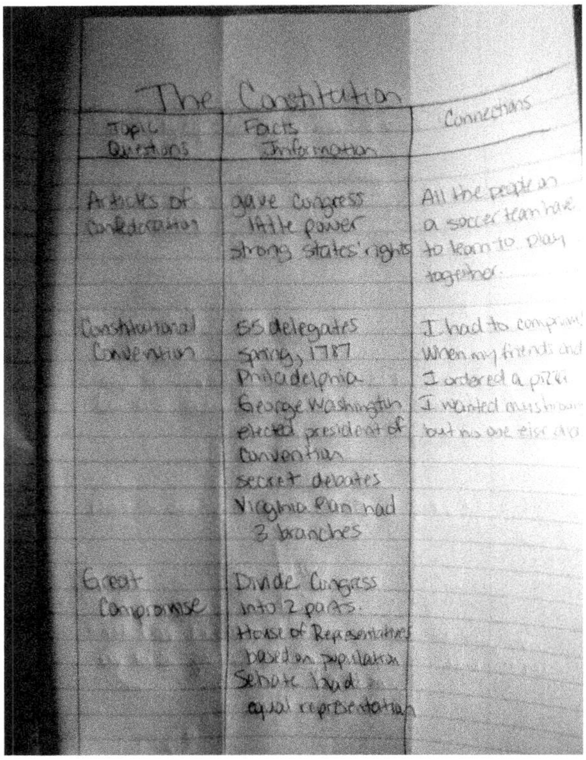

Figure 4.8: EXAMPLE OF THREE-COLUMN NOTES

The Cornell note-taking system is widely used and widely published. It was originally devised by Walter Pauk at Cornell University in the 1950s. It provides an organizational structure for anyone taking notes on any topic. It is similar in format to the two- and three-column notes. The template on page 54 provides students with an outline to follow. They can of course copy this template into their notebooks once they become familiar with it and know which information to record in each section.

Personal Connections

Besides note-taking, another way to keep students accountable for the information they learn from informational text or lectures is to have them reflect on and respond to the information from a personal perspective. Students can respond to information to reflect on how it relates to them (text-to-self), how it relates to events around them (text-to-world), or how it relates to other information or other texts they've read (text-to-text). The template on page 55 may help students organize their thinking when they first begin making personal connections. Another option is to have students simply reflect on the information freely in their social studies notebooks. **Figure 4.9** shows an example of a student recording her personal thoughts following a tour of the state capitol building.

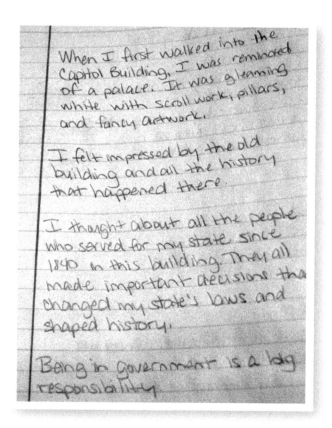

When I first walked into the Capitol Building, I was reminded of a palace. It was gleaming white with scroll work, pillars, and fancy artwork.

I felt impressed by the old building and all the history that happened there.

I thought about all the people who served for my state since 1840 in this building. They all made important decisions that changed my state's laws and shaped history.

Being in government is a big responsibility.

Figure 4.9: PERSONAL CONNECTIONS RECORDED AS A NOTEBOOK ENTRY

Sticky Notes

Sticky notes are perfect for those little memorable learning moments you want your students to capture while they are reading about a particular topic. They are small, relatively inexpensive, and extremely portable. You can take them outside the classroom for students to write on during simulation activities. You can even have students jot something down while they are walking down the hallway! Sticky notes are very versatile, and they serve many purposes when students are engaged in learning. **Figure 4.10** shows a class sticky note chart comparing how children's play differed between long ago and today.

stickball
ring and rolley hole
marbles
checkers

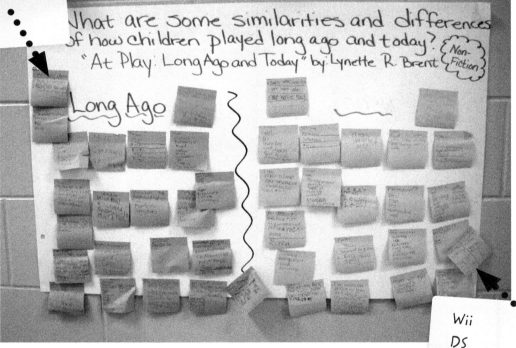

Wii
DS
Game Box
hopscotch
basketball

Figure 4.10: EXAMPLE OF STICKY NOTE POSTINGS COMPLETED AS A NOTE-TAKING STRATEGY DURING LEARNING

Graphic Organizers

Graphic organizers are another way students can take personalized notes to organize information during learning. This idea is presented in **Chapter 1** on page 8 and in this chapter on pages 36-37.

Adapting to Student Needs

Allow time for at-risk and ELL students to discuss their idea(s) with a partner before committing thoughts to paper. Also, these students could draw and label their ideas instead of writing entire sentences.

Have accelerated students create poster summaries or PowerPoint presentations to further summarize each concept. They should include definitions for relevant terms and examples, explain why this concept is important to understand, and perhaps also include one or two current events related to this topic.

Adding Technology

Have students work in small groups to conduct online research about a particular topic before reading about it. Have them summarize their findings in one or two paragraphs or share downloaded images in a PowerPoint presentation with the class. Then, have students compare the information they found online with information from the text selection.

Two-column Note-taking

Learning Template

Directions: Think about the information you learn while reading or listening. Record the main ideas or key points on the left side of the paper. Match these key points with details. Write these on the right side of the paper. Finally, summarize what all the information was about.

THESE ARE THE MAIN POINTS.	THIS INFORMATION SUPPORTS THE MAIN POINTS.
1.	1. 2. 3.
2.	1. 2. 3.
3.	1. 2. 3.

This is what I learned about _____ today.

Three-column Note-taking

Learning Template

Directions: Think about the information you learn while reading or listening. Record the main ideas or key points on the left side of the paper. Match these key points with details. Write these on the right side of the paper. Finally, summarize what all the information was about.

TOPIC OR QUESTION	INFORMATION AND FACTS	PERSONAL CONNECTION (I WONDER..., THIS MAKES ME THINK ABOUT..., THIS IS SIMILAR TO...)
1.	1. 2. 3.	
2.	1. 2. 3.	
3.	1. 2. 3.	
4.	1. 2. 3.	

Cornell Note-taking

Learning Template

Directions: Think about the information you learn while reading or listening. List the course name and date at the top. Record the main ideas or key points on the left side of the paper. Write related details and information to the right. Review the information. Write a one-paragraph summary at the bottom of the page.

Course Name and Date	
Main Ideas and Key Points	**Facts and Relevant Information (notes)**

Summary

My Personal Connections

Learning Template

Directions: Read a text selection about a topic. Then, think about how the information relates to you and the world around you. Record your thoughts and ideas here.

This information was about: _____

It came to me by (source) _____ on (date) _____

What was the information mostly about? _____
_____
_____

As you read, what did this remind you of? _____
_____
_____

As you read, how did the information make you feel? Why? _____
_____
_____

As you read, what did you imagine? _____
_____
_____

What is going on in the world around you that makes this information important?_____
_____
_____
_____

What surprising or interesting information did you learn while reading?
_____
_____
_____

If an alien visitor asked you about the information, what would you tell him? _____
_____
_____

CHAPTER FIVE

Writing while Learning Content:
Listening and Thinking in Social Studies

There are many more ways to learn about social studies concepts than by reading about them in textbooks, news articles, periodicals, or online informational sites. Students may also learn new information from videos, simulations, guest speakers, field trips, etc. Any of the previously mentioned reading strategies (see **Chapter 4**) work in listening situations as well. However, we teachers like to have more than one trick up our sleeves when supporting student learning. So, here are a few additional strategies you can use when students are listening to and thinking about social studies in the classroom.

Strategy 1: Taking Video and Lecture Notes

Integrated English Language Arts Skills: Main Idea and Details

Summary: Technology has come so far! Imagine where it will take us long after this book is published. Teachers and students have ready access to a slew of marvelous, appropriate, and interesting videos and audio-visual learning segments from a host of reputable online resources. There are too many to mention! I am sure you have your favorites. If you have not had the time to investigate for yourself, the websites in **Figure 5.1** provide quick access to just the right video you are looking for.

Teachers' Domain	www.teachersdomain.org
PBS	www.pbs.org
The History Channel	www.history.com/videos

Figure 5.1: WEBSITES WITH VIDEOS ON ALMOST ANY SOCIAL STUDIES TOPIC

While students are watching and listening, it's your job to hold students accountable for the information they were to have gleaned from either a video or lecture (or slideshow presentation). This can be accomplished by a simple writing task, such as having students summarize the information on a note card, which you collect and review to ensure adequate learning has taken place. Students can also take "free notes" in their notebooks, but without having practiced this particular skill, students tend to write nothing or everything. Depending on their age, grade level, intellectual ability, and prior practice, they may not have the mental aquity to listen, differentiate important ideas from non-important ideas, and synthesize these ideas in a written summary, all while the video or presentation is in continuous play. Surely, we want to lead students to this outcome. To help get them there, providing a graphic organizer, such as the note-taking graphic organizer on page 59, will help students stay focused on the main ideas of the audio-visual learning tool and support their thinking while the video continues to roll.

In addition to summary cards and graphic organizers, teachers can also use the sticky note idea (see page 50) or have students generate questions about the video. Whichever strategy is used, be sure to follow up the watching-and-listening activity with some effective learning strategy, such as the ones explained here or listed below.

Suggestions for Writing to Learn

1. Summarize the main idea of the video on a note card.

2. Record important points in notebooks.

3. Complete a ready-made graphic organizer. (See the table on page 37 for a list of graphic organizer resources.)

4. Complete a video-specific graphic organizer.

5. Conduct a class summary following the video. Have students record their ideas each on their own sticky note to post to a chart.

6. Have students write questions they still have about the information from the video.

7. Have students write quiz questions from the information presented in the video. Group students by fours or fives, and have them quiz each other using the notes they took.

8. Have students make up three truths and one lie using the information they obtained from the video. Ask selected students to share their statements. The class listens, using their own notes to identify the one lie among the truths.

What It Looks Like

Figure 5.2 shows an example of what a seventh grader might record in her notebook during a debate between two county commissioners regarding the use of protected land.

Bob Graves PRO	Helen Peabody AGAINST
- create jobs	- the land is protected by law for a reason
- the person who owns the land has the right to develop it	- the buildings are not appropriate for the area
- land use changes can and should happen to continue local growth	- there are water and sewer issues. The land is nearly impossible to build on
	- it will harm surrounding areas

Figure 5.2: LISTENING NOTES RECORDED AS A NOTEBOOK ENTRY

Figure 5.3 shows an example of a completed reflection following a video titled "Declaring Freedom...but for Whom?" from Teachers' Domain (**www.teachersdomain.org**). The organizer was created specifically for this particular video. It helps students compare the two perspectives, one of the author of the Declaration of Independence, and one of an historical expert. The questions require students to infer a good deal of information from the short clip. The organizer keeps them focused on the main points and allows them to reflect on their own ideas as they watch and listen.

PERSPECTIVE	HISTORICAL FIGURE	
	Thomas Jefferson	Colin Powell
How does this person view the principles of the Declaration of Independence?	*Thomas Jefferson wanted to define a distinctly American view of freedom.*	*"All men" should have meant ALL people, including blacks.*

TERM	DEFINITION	
	Thomas Jefferson's Definition	Colin Powell's Definition
unalienable rights	*Rights given to white men*	*Rights given to people by God*
liberty	*Freedom from tyranny*	*Personal freedom*

Whom did Thomas Jefferson mean by "all men" when he wrote, "All men are created equal?"

White, land-owning men

Colin Powell accuses Thomas Jefferson of violating the principles of the Declaration of Independence. Do you agree or disagree with Powell's accusation? Why or why not?

I think Powell unfairly accuses Jefferson because Jefferson lived in a different time when things were very different. Thomas Jefferson kept slaves, even though he wrote that all men are created equal. He had included statements in his original draft to end slavery, but they were deleted when the Declaration was revised. Today, "all men" means "all people," no matter what race they are or whether they are men or women. Thomas Jefferson kept slaves because that was how things were back then. Today, Jefferson would not have slaves.

What do you think Colin Powell would say to Thomas Jefferson were he alive today?

"Hey, dude, how can a slave owner justify that all men are created equal?"

Figure 5.3: Video notes

Adapting to Student Needs

Preview the video ahead of time. Write the main ideas along the left column of a two-column note-taking template for at-risk and ELL students. If additional scaffolding is needed, include one or two details for each main idea, and instruct these students to listen for the third detail to write on the line. Over time, scale back the scaffolding until students can complete this template without any assistance.

Accelerated students can research historians, geographers, economists, or other people who work in fields related to this topic. Allow them time to share the results of their research with the class, including photos of the people at work.

Adding Technology

As a summative assignment, have students work in small groups to write a script for their own documentary (video) about this topic. Use video-recording equipment such as a digital camera, video camera, or computer with webcam and a movie-making program (i.e., iMovie or Movie Maker) to record and publish student work.

Strategy 2: What Does This Mean to Me?

Integrated English Language Arts Skills: Drawing Conclusions; Personal Connections

Description: Students can take notes, complete graphic organizers, or write simple summaries when listening to and thinking about information. Another way to hold students accountable for the information they learn from a video, guest speaker, or real-life or virtual field trip is to have them reflect on and respond to the information from a personal perspective. This is similar to having students make text-to-self connections (see page 3), but students use other media from which to make connections.

Directions

1. Provide each student with a copy of the "My View" learning template on page 62.

2. Have students reflect on the main points of the information.

3. Students should complete the organizer independently.

4. Pair the students to have them share their thoughts.

5. As a class, discuss how the students made personal connections to the information.

What It Looks Like

The social studies notebook entry in **Figure 5.4** shows how a student can record her personal thoughts following a debate by two county commissioners on the topic of land use. This student recorded her personal opinion after hearing both sides of the issue. (This example is the second part of the student's notes displayed in **Figure 5.2**.)

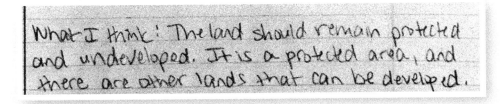

What I think: The land should remain protected and undeveloped. It is a protected area, and there are other lands that can be developed.

Figure 5.4: A STUDENT'S PERSONAL RESPONSE AS A NOTEBOOK ENTRY FOLLOWING A DEBATE

Adapting to Student Needs

Instead of writing and then sharing, have at-risk and ELL students share, then write. You might pull them together in a small group to discuss how the information related to them, and support their writing efforts by being available to answer questions, spell unknown words, or generate additional ideas to write. Also, these students could be allowed to first draw their thoughts, then use their illustrations as the starting point for their written ideas.

Accelerated students can make connections to other disciplines, such as math and science, or perhaps even band, art, or foreign languages. In the example in **Figure 4.9**, students might reference the height, width, and circumference of the dome in both standard and metric measures or explain Latin inscriptions encountered on the tour.

Adding Technology

Have students compare information about a particular topic from two sources, such as a video and a guest speaker or a real-life and a virtual tour. They can record similarities and differences between the two sources.

My View

Learning Template

Directions: Listen to information about a topic. Then, think about how the information relates to you and the world around you. Record your thoughts and ideas here.

This information was about: _____

It came to me by (source) _____ on (date) _____

What was the information mostly about? _____
_____
_____

As you listened, what did this remind you of? _____
_____
_____

As you listened, how did the information make you feel? Why? _____
_____
_____

As you listened, what did you imagine? _____
_____
_____

What is going on in the world around you that makes this information important? _____
_____
_____

What surprising or interesting information did you learn while listening? _____
_____
_____
_____

If an alien visitor asked you about the information, what would you tell him? _____
_____
_____
_____

Strategy 3: Analyzing Primary and Secondary Sources

Integrated English Language Arts Skills: Main Idea and Details; Cause and Effect; Compare and Contrast; Sequencing; Inference; Drawing Conclusions

Description: Students can gain information related to any number of social studies topics through text resources, speeches and lectures, field trips, videos, and interactive activities. They can also learn by analyzing primary and secondary sources. Primary sources are original documents or archives from the past. Examples include maps, documents, letters, reports, logs, eyewitness reports, and such. Secondary sources are accounts about primary sources. Examples include interpretations, biographies, opinion articles, and documentaries. Any information that comes to us secondhand is considered a secondary source.

As part of a complete review of history and historical events, students may be required by their state standards to review, analyze, and compare primary and secondary sources. The activities in this chapter require students to critically apply information, calling for them to make observations and inferences and draw conclusions. They can also analyze information, compare it to other sources, compare perspectives, and evaluate conclusions drawn from a particular source. This strategy provides an outlining tool for teachers to use when engaging their students with primary and secondary sources.

Directions

1. Provide each student with a copy of either the "Primary Source Review" or "Secondary Source Review" learning template on pages 65 or 67.

2. Have students review the primary or secondary source in pairs or as a small group.

3. Students should complete the organizer with their learning partners or teams.

4. As a class, discuss students' analyses. Compare the conclusions each group drew regarding the author's purpose of the document and their rating of the document as a useful and reliable source.

What It Looks Like

The example on page 66 shows how students may have completed the primary source outline after reviewing, analyzing, and discussing the government's use of posters to rally public support for the war effort (WWII).

Adapting to Student Needs

As students work in groups, have English speakers summarize the document(s) for ELL students, explaining in simpler terms what the information shows and why it was created. When reviewing several sources, both ELL students and at-risk students may benefit from their group creating a concept map of the information.

Accelerated students can average the groups' ratings for each source and compile the information in a graph for the class. This information, when shared with the class, provides a more quantitative analysis of the document(s), leading to further discussion regarding the usefulness and reliability of the sources. Students can discuss why one source may have achieved a higher rating than another source. Using this information, the class can then create an evaluation rubric to use when evaluating further sources to determine the usefulness, reliability, and validity of the information.

Adding Technology

Have students develop a word-processing document listing the best primary and secondary sources online. Attach this document to your website for students to access from home.

TEACHER TIP

Two Websites to Find Primary Sources

Library of Congress
www.loc.gov/index.html

National Archives
www.archives.gov

Primary Source Review

Learning Template

Directions: Look at and analyze a primary source. Use this page to organize ideas related to the primary source.

Title: _____

Author: _____

Date Originated: _____ Place Originated: _____

Author's Intended Audience:_____

Purpose of Document: _____

_____

What is this document mostly about, or what information does it explain? _____

_____

_____

Who or what is mentioned in the document? _____

_____

_____

Why did the author include these people, places, things, or ideas? _____

_____

_____

How useful is this source as a document to learn about the past? (circle)

5 – extremely   4 – very   3 – somewhat   2 – not very   1 – not at all

Explain why you rated this source the way you did. _____

_____

_____

What did you learn from reviewing this source? _____

_____

_____

_____

_____

Primary Source Review

Student Example

Directions: Look at and analyze a primary source. Use this page to organize ideas related to the primary source.

Title: _"Powers of Persuasion — Poster Art of World War II" from the National Archives_

Author: _Different artists_

Date Originated: _WWII era_   Place Originated: _unknown_

Author's Intended Audience: _Men and women living in the United States during WWII_

Purpose of Document: _To persuade American civilians that they can support the war effort even though they are not fighting overseas and to rally support for the war effort_

What is this document mostly about, or what information does it explain? _The posters show how American muscle, women, African Americans, rationing, and valuing freedom will help win the war._

Who or what is mentioned in the document? _Muscular men with torpedoes, women saluting and showing strength, African Americans working in factories and in uniform, different ways to ration and conserve needed materials, the value of purchasing war bonds, and people valuing freedom from fear_

Why did the author include these people, places, things, or ideas? _They showed that all Americans had a place in helping the war effort._

How useful is this source as a document to learn about the past? (circle)

5 – extremely   (4 – very)   3 – somewhat   2 – not very   1 – not at all

Explain why you rated this source the way you did. _I learned a lot about how the government rallied Americans to do their part to support WWII. They made me feel patriotic, strong, and involved, even though I wasn't around during that time. I feel proud that my great-grandparents were part of the war effort, even though they were not in the army._

What did you learn from reviewing this source? _Everyone had a part in the war effort, even if they were not fighting overseas. The posters were very persuasive and used people's patriotism to encourage them to become and stay involved. They probably made everyone feel important._

Secondary Source Review

Learning Template

Directions: Look at and analyze a secondary source. Use this page to organize ideas related to the secondary source.

Title: _____

Author: _____

Date Originated: _____ Place Originated: _____

Author's Intended Audience: _____

Purpose of Source: _____

_____

What is this document mostly about, or what information does it explain? _____

_____

_____

What did you learn from reviewing this source? _____

_____

_____

_____

What is the author's purpose for writing this source? _____

_____

_____

What personal opinions does the author include, or how does the author lead the reader to a certain conclusion? _____

_____

_____

Do you agree with the author's opinions? Explain. _____

_____

_____

How reliable is this source as a document to learn about the past? (circle)

_____

5 – extremely   4 – very   3 – somewhat   2 – not very   1 – not at all

Explain why you rated this source the way you did. _____

_____

_____

CHAPTER SIX

Writing to Extend Learning

Up to this point in a particular unit of study, students have engaged in content; learned essential and specific vocabulary; deeply explored, studied, and read about ideas and information; and written to reflect on, absorb, respond to, and internalize their learning. Now students can apply and extend their learning in a unique or novel situation or to learn additional information related to the topic. Extensions of learning allow additional time for students to explore ideas, processes, concepts, and skills to further the learning experience. This is also an opportunity for students to clarify any lingering misunderstandings they may have about the topic.

Examples of extension activities include playing or creating board or trivia games, participating in simulations, watching or creating documentaries, making models or examples, completing a WebQuest, conducting a research project, or linking content to real-world applications. As with any other stage of the learning process, students need time to process new and related information, record their personal thoughts and ideas, and make meaningful connections to the content. All of this can be accomplished by having students write about their learning experiences. The following pages provide simple and effective extension ideas that require students to demonstrate their extended learning through writing.

Strategy 1: Writing to Complete Projects, Problems, and Prompts

One strategy for having students extend their learning is to assign them a project, problem, or writing prompt. These can all be completed independently or in pairs or small groups. Essentially, students are provided a written task related to what they have been studying, and they complete it.

Projects might include research reports (see pages 69-72), WebQuests (see pages 78-79), or the construction of a three-dimensional model or example. Teachers should hold students accountable for all of these extension ideas by requiring some written component in addition to the project itself. For example, if students build a three-dimentional model of a geographical area, they should also be required to write a summary explaining how this model represents the land.

Problems set students to the task of resolving some conflict. Simulations (see pages 76-77) are perfect for this purpose. Some WebQuests, too, engage students in resolving conflicts or problem solving to accomplish some goal.

Prompts sound boring, but they do not have to be. Consider this writing prompt:

You are a reporter for a southern newspaper in the mid- to early 1800s. The cotton gin has revolutionized the cotton industry! You decide to get two points of view on the matter of slavery in light of this invention. You interview a southern plantation owner and Nat Turner. Write three interview questions for each person and the responses he may have given from his perspective.

With this example, students must use what they learned about the growth of the cotton industry (and, consequently, the slave industry) in the South and events related to the North's rise against slavery. Instead of an interview, students could write a script for a movie, including characters, setting, and dialogue. You, as the social studies teacher, uncover the learning students truly captured by having them write to a prompt like this. Students get to put all their language arts training into practice, and everyone gets entertained by whatever summaries are created.

Regardless of the project, problem, or prompt assigned to students, hold them accountable for their task by providing them with a copy of the **Project or Problem Rating Scale** (page 96) or **Prompt Rubric** (page 95). Be sure students are aware of how their work will be evaluated *before* they begin working.

Strategy 2: Writing Research Projects

Integrated English Language Arts Skills: Planning; Research; Summarizing

Description: Classroom time restraints may require extension activities be assigned as homework or outside class time. Or, for extensive research projects, students might spend some class time completing their work while only some of the work is completed outside of class. One way to research more in a short amount of time is to divide and conquer. Assign each small group of students one smaller component of a larger research project. The goups can then combine their information into one complete project.

Be aware that research projects tend to engage students in the low-level skills of knowledge and comprehension. We like to think that we are requiring students to synthesize information, a high-level skill, but this is not the case. Synthesis requires original thought in a novel and unique situation. Regurgitating facts and information from others' published work is simply a summarizing task. Compare this with a summary students might write from participating in a simulation (see pages 76-77). When students write their summary, they must start with only the information they gathered through their experiences. This work is completely synthesized by the student.

To elevate the cognitive level of a typical research project, you might consider requiring students to include a statement or to explain why this information is important to know or how these facts apply to their community. Another idea is to have students write the report from the perspective of an historian in this field. Or, you could have students change their report into a persuasive essay. Additionally, the ideas on pages 76-77 include examples of three motivating projects students might complete to culminate a unit of study on elections, historical people, and ancient civilizations.

Directions

1. Have students select a topic to research. Provide suggestions for appropriate and interesting topics, if needed.

2. Make one copy of the "Research Project" learning template for each student (page 72).

3. Provide guidelines for conducting research. Inform students of specific criteria, such as how many references to site or include, the format you prefer (typed or handwritten), and whether they should include pictures, illustrations, or diagrams.

4. Specific criteria such as that listed in step three will affect the evaluation rubric you use to assess student work. Make the necessary adjustments to the rubric. You can modify the **Research Report Rubric** on page 94 or make your own.

5. Give students a copy of the evaluation rubric. Review it with them. Be sure they understand how their work will be evaluated.

6. If possible, reserve class time for students to conduct their research, organize their ideas, and write their first draft. Conference with students regarding their progress. You might also consider establishing completion goals with the class (research completed by a certain date, first draft completed by a certain date, etc.). Be sure students are aware of the deadline for completion, and the consequences for submitting late work.

What It Looks Like

Reports come in all shapes and sizes, from murals to posters to typed or handwritten reports. As students begin to develop their ideas for their research project, guide them to decide upon the best medium through which to publish their work. Some projects may be best completed as a typed report. Others may be better completed using video-recording equipment, such as when students conduct an interview with an historical figure. If you're not choosey about the format of the project, allow students the freedom to conceive and develop their own ideas. If you would rather everyone submit a typed report, make your expectations clear before students begin researching.

Adapting to Student Needs

Make time daily for conferencing with at-risk and ELL students regarding their progress. Support their efforts by suggesting or finding text resources at suitable readability levels. You might also provide additional graphic organizers for them to complete to help them organize their ideas.

Accelerated students can complete alternatives to traditional reports by organizing their information in any one of the following formats:

- ABC book: a composite of pages with each page highlighting a key term that begins with each subsequent letter of the alphabet: abolitionist, border state, confederacy, etc.

- article for a scientific journal or newspaper

- diary entries from the perspective of the person they are researching

- interview with the person they are researching

- radio report

- scrapbook

- technical manual

- webpages

Adding Technology

Be sure to require students to use the World Wide Web to conduct at least some of their research. This is also an opportune moment in your students' education to discuss which websites are best for research purposes and which are not. Conduct a lesson on finding and using reliable Internet resources, or ask for assistance with this from your school or district's technology department. Show students how to cite these types of resources (in addition to text resources) appropriately.

Allow students to make a podcast or digitally edited video of their project. Both iMovie and Movie Maker are suitable video-editing programs for students.

Research Project

Learning Template

Topic: _____

_____

Purpose for writing: Why are you writing this paper? _____

_____

Conduct your research. Use other paper or note cards. Write facts and information you believe are important. Be sure to reference your facts. You should be able to find the information quickly if asked.

Organize your ideas. Group the information you found. Decide on the main ideas. Then, list the details that support each main idea.

MAIN IDEA 1	MAIN IDEA 2	MAIN IDEA 3
DETAILS	DETAILS	DETAILS

Write your first draft. Use notebook paper or a word-processing program. Write freely. Do not be concerned about grammar, punctuation, spelling, or capital letters just yet. Write to get all the information down on the page.

Review your work. Re-read your whole report. Make sure you included all the important information. Make revisions as needed.

Edit your work. Now you can check spelling, grammar, punctuation, and capital letters. Each paragraph should be indented. Fix what you need to fix.

Write your final draft. This is your final product. It should be neat and organized and include all essential information. This one counts! Take pride in your work.

Strategy 3: Conducting Historical Inquiry

Integrated English Language Arts Skills: Research; Summarizing; Inference; Drawing Conclusions

Description: Historical inquiry combines the best of research and simulation. Its purpose is to "bridge the gap between research and practice in terms of preparing teachers and students to engage in the doing of history" (The Historical Inquiry Project, 2005). Contrary to learning a series of facts and information, students instead analyze historical sources and develop historical accounts. They reach their own plausible conclusions from analyzing and interpreting several sources and use this historical evidence to provide answers to historical questions. For example, students can review, analyze, and interpret a letter from Bobby Murray to the Children's Bureau (1939) in an attempt to answer the question, "What was the life of a child like during the Depression?" (This historical inquiry is available at **www.historicalinquiry.com/scim/demonstration.cfm**.)

The Historical Inquiry Project clarifies the process of historical inquiry by identifying five steps for students to follow as they conduct their inquiry. The steps to a successful historical inquiry following this "SCIM-C" method are listed in **Figure 6.1**.

STEP	ACTIONS
Summarizing	Examine sources; determine the subject, author, purpose, audience, and type; identify facts, dates, ideas, opinions, and perspectives
Contextualizing	Clarifying historical language, meanings, values, habits, and customs of the time period
Inferring	Make inferences within the context of the text
Monitoring	Question and clarify initial conclusions
Corroborating	Verify initial conclusions through multiple sources

Figure 6.1: STEPS TO THE SCIM-C METHOD OF INSTRUCTION

Directions

1. Make one copy of the "Historical Inquiry" learning template (page 75).

2. Write a question for students to answer on the lines provided.

3. Make enough copies of the learning template for each pair or small group of students.

4. Provide each pair or small group of students with a copy of the primary source document(s).

5. Have students use the learning template to guide their historical inquiry. Students should summarize their conclusions using additional paper, if needed, or in their notebooks.

6. As a class, compare the conclusions each group drew from their historical inquiry. Discuss similarities and differences among the conclusions. Clarify students' statements. Be sure they did not state their own personal opinions but instead used facts and information to write an objective statement.

Adapting to Student Needs

Work with ELL and at-risk students in small groups to help them analyze the documents, especially clarifying language and customs of the time period.

Accelerated students can use the document(s) to create an eyewitness account of the events as a news report or an interview.

Adding Technology

Have students use movie-making software such as iMovie or Movie Maker to piece together a complete news report with live, on-the-scene interviews.

Historical Inquiry

Learning Template

Directions: Review a primary source document. Use it to try to answer the question below. Use this page to analyze and interpret this document. Draw your conclusions.

Question to answer: _____

Subject of document: _____

Author: _____

Type of document: _____

Purpose of document: _____

Intended audience: _____

FACTS	
DATES	
IDEAS	
OPINIONS/ PERSPECTIVES	

What is different about the language from the time period of this document when compared to today's language? _____

What customs are different between then and now? _____
_____

How do the differences in society change how you interpret this document? _____
_____

What conclusions can you draw from this document as you attempt to answer the question?
_____
_____

What other documents might provide more insight and help you answer the question better?
_____
_____

Strategy 4: Participating in Simulations

Integrated English Language Arts Skills: Drawing Conclusions; Inference; Cause and Effect

Description: A simulation walks students through a fictional replicated event as it might happen or did happen in the past. Examples include conducting a mock trial or mock election. The use of simulations in the social sciences is a valued, semi-authentic, and meaningful way for students to engage in historical, geographical, economic, and civic models and experiences. Students make predictions about cause-effect relationships, and they make decisions that influence the outcomes of events. They increase the understanding students have of processes, events, and periods in time related to any number of topics in social studies.

While simulations themselves may provide engaging opportunities for students to more closely experience history, they also provide meaningful opportunities for students to record their progress through time in writing. The most obvious writing strategy to use with simulations is to have students keep a personal log of their trials and tribulations, reflecting on their learning and how they may have acted differently had they known the outcome ahead of time. Other writing strategies to use with simulations are listed in **Figure 6.2**.

Writing Strategies to Use with Simulations

Personal journals or logs	Postcards
Timelines	Greeting cards
Advice columns	Friendly or business letters
Almanacs	Headlines
Newspaper articles	Horoscopes
Calendars	Newscasts
Dialogue journals	Interviews
Posters	Scrapbooks

Figure 6.2: WRITING TO SUPPORT SIMULATIONS

What It Looks Like

The ideas listed in **Figure 6.3** show how some of the writing strategies listed on the previous page can be natural extensions of simulation activities.

ACTIVITY	OBJECTIVE	WRITING STRATEGIES
Classroom elections simulation	Students act to get their candidate elected class president	Campaign posters Campaign speeches Polling updates/newscasts Candidate biographies Campaign strategy proposals and presentations Acceptance speeches Interviews
Needs and wants simulation	Students learn how advertising plays a critical role in shaping peoples' needs and wants	Advertising proposals and presentations Advertising posters Advertisements (visual and audio) Evaluations and feedback of advertisements Learning logs related to needs and wants
Mock trial	Students participate as the plaintiff, defendant, attorneys, witnesses, and jurors to experience how the American judicial system works	Trial preparations Opening and closing statements Dialogue, testimony, and depositions Court reports Media interviews Headlines and newspaper articles

Figure 6.3: EXAMPLES OF SIMULATIONS IN THE SOCIAL SCIENCES AND THEIR CONNECTION TO WRITING

Adapting to Student Needs

Provide choices of writing assignments to ELL and at-risk students based on their experiences, abilities, and language acquisition. Or, assign simpler tasks to them, and provide needed outlines and graphic organizers to help them plan and execute their writing.

Accelerated students can search current newspapers and other media for connections from the past to the present. Have them share their findings with the class, summarizing how the current event relates to the classroom simulation.

Adding Technology

Have students take digital photos of the simulation in progress. Compose a class account of the simulation and the outcomes as they unfold using slideshow or movie-making software such as iMovie or Movie Maker. Summarize each day's events and include corresponding photos of the activities.

Strategy 5: Participating in WebQuests

Integrated English Language Arts Skills: Main Idea and Details; Summarizing; Vocabulary Development; Drawing Conclusions; Inference; Cause and Effect; Compare and Contrast

Description: WebQuests were pioneered by Bernie Dodge at San Diego State University in 1995. Since then, they have developed into a highly effective instructional strategy for encouraging collaboration and integrating technology. During a WebQuest, students are assigned various tasks using online or virtual resources to create an overall product. An effective WebQuest is well-structured, guides students through the inquiry process, provides access to appropriate and useful websites, and encourages choice, collaboration, and novelty throughout each stage of completion. WebQuests naturally lend themselves to writing in the content areas. They set students to a specific task, requiring them to use and reflect on online resources to accomplish some objective. For example, in the "Searching for China" WebQuest (**tommarch.com/learning/ChinaWebQuest1.html**), students analyze five cultural and geographical components of China, then use their information to create one visual image of China to reflect their learning. The author of this WebQuest, Tom March, suggests the following writing projects to culminate this activity:

- Create a travel infomercial to persuade people to visit China.

- Create a slideshow to impressively portray China.

- Create a game show to challenge people regarding information about China.

Directions

1. Search online for a WebQuest related to an upcoming unit of study. Find one that meets the criteria listed in the previous paragraphs. The websites listed in **Figure 6.4** offer a starting point for teachers interested in using WebQuests as an engaging and effective instructional tool.

2. Divide the class into heterogeneous groups. The size of the group will depend on the number of tasks embedded in the WebQuest and the abilities of the students in the groups.

3. Review the WebQuest with the class. Clarify the groups' objectives. Also clarify your expectations for the level of each student's participation within the group. Every student should have a task to contribute to the group project. In some cases, more than one person may work on the same task. Even so, everyone has a role.

4. Allow time for students to access the online information, gather their research, and complete their part of the overall group project. Be sure to include a written component if the WebQuest does not have one built in.

5. Allow time for the groups to assemble and complete the overall WebQuest objective(s). If desired, set aside class time for students to share their projects.

6. Modify the **Project or Problem Rating Scale** on page 96 to reflect specific criteria for evaluating student work.

What It Looks Like

A WebQuest sets small groups of students to a specific task. Students access online resources to complete the tasks, so everyone needs access to computers and the Internet. Everyone should have a contributing part to the larger group project. Students should have a clear understanding before they begin of how their work will be evaluated, and whether they will be evaluated as a group, as an individual, or through some combination of both their individual efforts and the group product. This criteria should be spelled out in the evaluation rubric.

Starting Points: WebQuest Websites

WebQuest.org	www.webquest.org/index.php
EdTechTeacher	www.edtechteacher.org/webquests.html
BestWebQuests.com	www.bestwebquests.com

Figure 6.4: WEBQUEST WEBSITES

Strategy 6: Writing to Engage in Debate

Integrated English Language Arts Skills: Main Idea and Details; Summarizing; Vocabulary Development; Drawing Conclusions; Inference; Cause and Effect

Description: Historians, politicians, government officials, sociologists, anthropologists, and other experts in the social science fields all have their own personal views regarding facts, information, and events. They always seem to be willing to share their views with the public and engage in healthy debate with other experts and everyday citizens. The "Opinion Statements" (page 9) and "What Does This Mean to Me?" (page 60) strategies in this book provide students opportunities to formulate their own opinions regarding matters of historical importance.

Therefore, students can also engage in the highly effective instructional strategy of debate.

According to Amy Azzam (2008), debates are one high-yield strategy that teach critical thinking and literacy, develop students' organizational and research skills, promote self-confidence and, most importantly, empower students by ensuring they have a voice. Azzam argues that "debate has a better chance than many other school activities of turning adolescents into good thinkers, good researchers, good speakers, and good citizens" (p. 69).

Debates require students to write persuasively from one point of view. They must think abstractly, synthesizing information to formulate a rational, justified, and plausible perspective intended to persuade others to "their side." This is a high-level instructional strategy that inherently requires students to apply their creative writing skills to accomplish a specific objective through writing.

Directions

1. Decide upon a topic to debate. Or, assign different pairs of students different topics to debate.

2. Make one copy of the "Point of View" learning template on page 81 for each student. With his or her partner, each student should decide on one opposing point of view.

3. Allow time for students to research their topic and write their arguments.

4. Provide adequate time for students to conduct their debate. Set time limits, if needed.

5. Use the evaluation rubric on page 95 to assess students regarding both their written work and their speaking skills.

What It Looks Like

An effective debate is passionate and intense yet thoughtful and respectful. When students stand to debate, be sure to set ground rules or create them as a class. For example, yelling and shouting should be prohibited, as well as displaying negative body language, such as sighing or rolling one's eyes. Decide if you will have a moderator, and consider a written class follow-up. This might be a pre- and post-poll regarding the issue up for debate or a personal reflection of the experience in their social studies notebooks.

Adapting to Student Needs

Allow ELL and at-risk students to play to their strengths. Some at-risk students may not be able to effectively put their ideas to paper, but they may be excellent speakers. If this is the case, allow them to use outlines instead of whole summaries, relying on a few key terms to state their case. Instead of debating, ELL and at-risk students could participate by acting as the moderators. Provide at-risk students with a script to follow to start, guide, and conclude the debate.

Adding Technology

Videotape the debates for students to watch at a later time. Have them evaluate their own performance based on facts, information, persuasive techniques, presentation, and style. Use their personal reflections as part of the evaluation process.

Point of View

Learning Template

Directions: Use this page to help organize facts and information for a debate. Then, use additional paper to write a persuasive essay.

Topic: _____

My point of view: _____

Consider facts (including past events, statistics, and information), opinions, and biases or stereotypes that support your point of view. Use persuasive techniques such as bandwagon, societal pressure, and scare tactics to write your arguments. Each argument should have adequate support.

Argument 1:	Support
Argument 2:	Support
Argument 3:	Support

Use your arguments and support to write your persuasive essay.

CHAPTER SEVEN

Writing Strategies to Assess and Evaluate Student Learning

Finally. A social studies unit has come to a close. Students have discussed, reflected, analyzed, comprehended, considered, evaluated, compared, connected, and synthesized information. Now, we have to have a way to evaluate their learning—quantify it in some way for a grade.

There are many theories on evaluating and grading student work. You likely have your system in place and are quite satisfied with it. But, does it truly reflect the level of understanding students can demonstrate for a particular topic and the concepts, content, and skills contained within it? If grading and evaluating student work is a topic of interest to you, and you want to learn more about it, you might consider reading any of these three resources:

- *Ahead of the Curve: The Power of Assessment to Transform Teaching and Learning*. Edited by Douglas Reeves. Published by Solution Tree, 2007.

- *Classroom Assessment & Grading that Work*. Written by Robert J. Marzano. Published by the Association for Supervision and Curriculum Development (ASCD), 2006.

- *Educative Assessment: Designing Assessments to Inform and Improve Student Performance*. Written by Grant Wiggins. Published by Jossey-Bass, 1998.

The ideas in this book have not addressed any particular social studies topic (*what* students should know), but they did provide strategies for supporting student learning (*how* students learn) through proven instructional strategies. This chapter explores ideas and suggestions for determing whether students reached a disirable outcome (whether they "got it"). Regardless of your process for grading, the ideas in this chapter provide strategies for determining students' levels of understanding through writing.

Strategy 1: Writing to Review Content

Before administering a final assessment, students can use writing to review the content they have spent so much time learning. A review is simply an opportunity for students to look over, reflect upon, study, or re-examine facts and information. The simple act of re-reading notes taken throughout the course of study might be an effective review strategy for some students. But add the formal act of writing to review, and more students will be mentally engaged in the act of studying. These three ideas engage students' minds as they prepare for a test, project, or written summary of their learning.

Concept Acrostic

This activity encourages collaboration. It is active and fast-paced, and it involves everyone, regardless of skill level. Simply list a main concept vertically on a sheet of chart paper. Do this for each group of five to six students. Post the charts. Give each group one marker. Each group lines up, facing its chart. When you say, "Go," the first person in line uses any one of the letters of the concept as the first letter of a sentence related to the topic. Then, he or she passes the marker to the next person in line. Teams can use notes, text, information posted around the room, or any other means to generate a factual sentence. Play ends when all groups have written sentences for every letter. Then, groups can share their information with the class. **Figures 7.1 and 7.2** show how one group of fifth graders reviewed information about the thirteen original colonies and the American Revolution. Both topics (colonial America and the American Revolution) were abbreviated to make this particular activity more manageable for students.

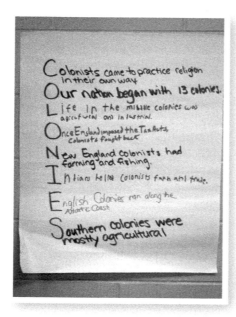 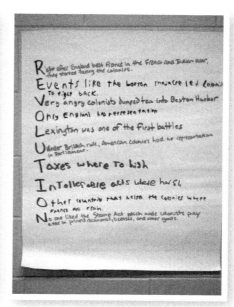

Figures 7.1 and 7.2: CONCEPT ACROSTIC REVIEW POSTERS RELATED TO COLONIAL AMERICA AND THE AMERICAN REVOLUTION

Quiz Games

Quiz games or quiz shows are highly motivating review strategies that fit any topic. They can be simple in design or highly complex, modeled after any favorite television or online competition. To get started, have students write questions and answers related to the topic on note cards. If desired, you can have them write a combination of low-level and high-level questions. (This should be modeled for students first.) Divide the class into teams, recite the rules or expectations, and start play. Be sure every student has an opportunity to respond to at least one question. English language learners can participate by keeping score. You might consider using some of the questions the students generate in the final assessment.

Question Cube

This strategy gets students talking and writing as they review essential information. Make one copy of the question cube on page 85 for each small group or pair of students. Then, have each student divide a sheet of notebook paper into six spaces. Each student, in turn, rolls the cube. A team member asks the appropriate question using his or her notes or text. For example, if a student rolls "Where?," a team member might ask "Where did the Aztecs build their capital city?" Then, the person who rolled must write the answer (in a complete sentence) in one of the six spaces. Play ends once all the students have written the answers to six questions. Students can then use their responses as an additional study aide.

Question Cube Outline

Teacher Note: Use this template with the "Question Cube" strategy described on page 84.

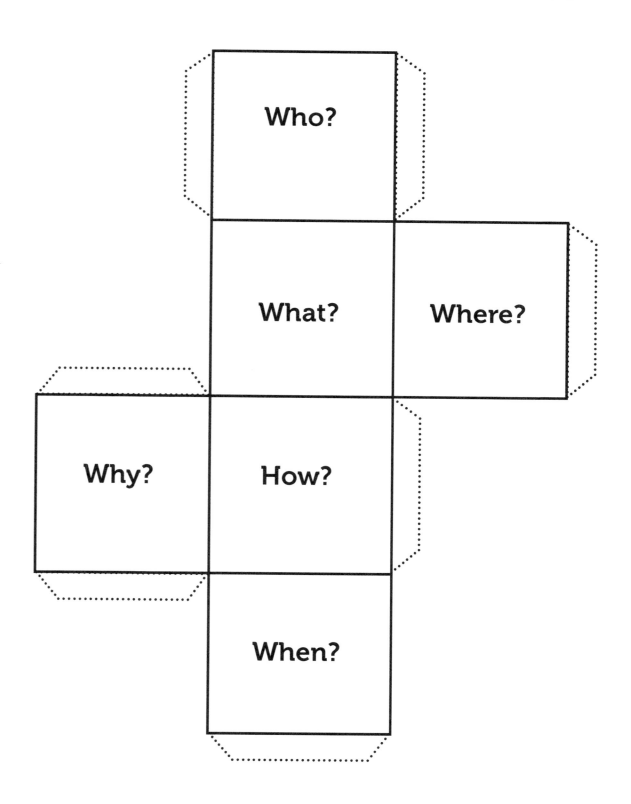

Strategy 2: Writing for the Purpose of Formative Assessments

Hopefully, teachers do not wait until the end of a unit to discover whether students have learned the facts, information, and ideas required by their standards and benchmarks. By then, it is too late. Formative assessments occur throughout the learning process, starting with an informal assessment of student misconceptions and prior knowledge before teaching even begins. This allows teachers to make adjustments to the teaching process, thereby allowing students who need additional instruction and activity to truly learn a particular topic or concept to have the time they need. The following suggestions will help teachers determine whether students are on track to meet the objectives of the unit before a summative, end-of-unit assessment occurs.

Notebook Review

This book started with an overview of the use of notebooks throughout a unit of study (see **Chapter 1**). As students record and respond in their notebooks, teachers can easily monitor students' understanding and thinking by simply walking around as students write, checking a notebook here or there, or by collecting notebooks for review weekly. Not every notebook needs a review every day or on one certain day. Break up the task by monitoring or collecting just five or six notebooks each day. By the end of the week, every student will have had his or her record-keeping checked.

Exit Cards

If checking notebooks is not feasible, have students respond to the information presented on exit cards once weekly. This is a simple strategy which allows you to guage students' levels of understanding of a particular topic with minimal resources, and it takes just five minutes at the end of class one day. Distribute a note card to each student, preferably one that is blank on one side and lined on the other. Pose a question or simple task to students such as "Explain Manifest Destiny" or "If you were King George, what message would you send to the colonists?" Students can use the blank side of the card to illustrate their ideas, then use the lined side to write an explanation. The cards do not allow for a lot of writing, so checking for formative purposes may be accomplished in a short amount of time.

One-sentence Summary

Another alternative to exit cards is to have students write a one-sentence summary on a strip of notebook paper. A question as simple as "What did you learn today?" will provide insights regarding students' initial understandings. A one-sentence summary sounds very simple. However, this can pose quite a challenge for some students. Before setting students to this task, provide one or two examples on the board or allow students to think aloud with a neighbor before putting pencil to paper.

Before and During Learning   Chapters **2** through **6** shared ideas to help students learn through writing before and throughout a unit of study. With each day came some opportunity for students to demonstrate their understanding through writing. Teachers can use their students' daily work as a means to assess whether they are grasping the ideas presented in the unit of study as it progresses. For example, the student who completed the key word prediction on page 19 adequately compared her definition to her neighbor's, and she included the true definition in her comparison. A quick review of the class's comparisons would have provided valuable information regarding students' grasp of the concept of *citizen* before the unit continued.

Quiz Me   Students do not necessarily need to complete a long, formal test to demonstrate their learning during a unit of study. Instead, short, deliberate quizzes may provide teachers adequate feedback related to where students are in the learning process. Multiple-choice quizzes are one option, but they generally do not encompass a wide enough range of concepts, nor are they long enough for students to truly demonstrate what they know and don't know. And, one never really knows if students are guessing or if they really do know the answer. Instead, consider using any of the writing strategies from any chapter in this book to determine how far students have come with regard to their learning. For example, you might post a list of related terms and have students group them on a sheet of paper and justify their categories. A quick check will inform you whether students have really learned the words or whether they remain a little lost. Or, have students complete a main idea/details or compare/contrast graphic organizer using their notes about a particular topic. Notes are supposed to provide students with a reflection of learning. If they can't accomplish this simple task given this level of support, students have not really grasped the main concepts you are trying to teach them.

If students seem off track at any point during a lesson or unit, or if they do not respond as thoroughly as you would have hoped, take the opportunity to re-teach this particular concept. You could engage students in a pair-share activity, video, conversation, or other simple activity to allow them additional time to explore a particular idea and revisit their understanding of the topic or concept. Or, the *extension* stage of a lesson is also an opportunity for students to "practice social studies" (see **Chapter 6**). Provide students with additional learning opportunities to support their understandings and extend and revise their thinking through writing.

Strategy 3: Writing for the Purpose of Summative Assessments

At the end of a unit comes some form of summative assessment. This is a culminating evaluation regarding the information, topics, and concepts students were to have learned from a comprehensive unit. End-of-chapter tests are summative assessments. State tests are summative assessments. They encompass a wide range of objectives and are usually formatted as multiple-choice, matching, or fill-in-the-blank questions. These types of questions are easy to score, but they usually do not require students to do a whole lot of thinking. If a student answers "c" (the correct answer) to question sixteen, do you really know that the student understood this idea, or did he perhaps guess well?

These suggestions offer a more in-depth look into students' comprehensive learning. They all require students to write to respond. Through students' written responses, you can get a true glimpse into their thoughts and depth of comprehension of subject matter.

Tell Me Why

A simple strategy to elevate students' thinking during guess-and-check tests is to have them explain off to the side *how* they knew "c" was the correct answer. Or, even more challenging, they can explain how they knew "a", "b," or "d" were *not* the correct answers. You can choose any one or two questions for students to respond to in this fashion or allow students to choose their own. It is not a daunting task for students to write to explain their thinking to one or two questions, and it is not a daunting task for teachers to grade all these summaries. Using a simple scale of zero to four is sufficient (see **Figure 7.3**).

4-Point Scale for Grading Written Response Questions

0 – No understanding

1 – Minimal understanding

2 – Partial understanding

3 – Some understanding

4 – Thorough understanding

Figure 7.3: FOUR-POINT RATING SCALE

Storyline

Another summative assessment idea is to have students write a realistic story, poem, song, article, tribute, folktale, or science-fiction story about the main topic from a unit of study, using all the related terms they encountered as part of their script. Use the **Prompt Rubric** on page 95 to evaluate student work. Be sure students understand that the clarity of their ideas will provide the feedback you need regarding their understanding. For example, students cannot simply list people like Meriwether Lewis and William Clark in their poems. If they are writing a limerick about these explorers' expedition west, they must include facts and information that are relevant and meaningful to their journey.

Strategy 4: Project-based Outcomes

Performance tasks, or project-based assignments, provide an alternative to traditional tests. When these assignments are formatted and developed correctly, teachers can determine how well their students understood a particular topic or concept. The benefit of performance tasks is that they allow students the freedom to be creative, reach out beyond the facts, and really demonstrate their learning through personal and individualized means. The biggest drawback to performance-based measures is that they are typically much more time consuming than tests for both students and teachers, and they require more extensive planning, resources, and materials than traditional paper-and-pencil tests.

Additionally, some projects, such as the construction of three-dimensional models or dioramas, do not inherently lend themselves to a writing task. Teachers might be able to see, literally, how their students interpret particular details with these types of projects. But they might not be able to really gauge the level of student learning. Fortunately, this dilemma is easily corrected by requiring summaries through display cards, book jackets, debates, descriptions, flip books, memos, audio recordings, reviews, or brochures, to name a few.

When developing performance tasks, Grant Wiggins (1998) cautions teachers to ensure their authenticity, credibility or validity, and high level of engagement. He suggests these simplified steps to developing such assessment activities (p. 147):

1. Think of or find an activity to use to assess a particular [objective] or set of objectives.

2. If this activity cannot validly and reliably assess the objectives, modify it so that it can.

3. Determine the criteria needed to complete the activity.

4. Develop a rubric to reflect the criteria and target objectives.

5. Evaluate the design of the task. Be sure it is engaging, is worth the time and energy to complete it, provides regular intervals of feedback for students, allows for an appropriate amount of latitude on the part of the student for completion, has clear directions and expectations, and will provide useful feedback regarding students' learning.

Following are three examples of performance tasks students might complete to culminate a unit related to elections, any unit with historic figures, and ancient civilizations. The **Project or Problem Rating Scale** on page 96 is generic but provides suggested criteria upon which to evaluate student work, and it leaves room for you to write in the specific criteria you want to see. When assigning larger projects, you may want to use the rubric provided as a guide and include more specific criteria related to the objectives of the unit and the project as part of the overall evaluation. For example, in the first project, you might include criteria evaluating the effectiveness of the advertisement tactics and their appeal to the public.

Sample Project-based Assessments

VOTE NOW!

Your local elections office has reported that voter turnout in your area has been declining over the years. This is an important election year! They need help boosting interest in voting and improving voter turnout.

Plan an advertising strategy with at least two tactics to improve voter turnout in your area. First, think of a motto or slogan you can chant at pep rallies and on the streets around town. Then, decide the best way to reach the most people. Maybe a television ad or repeated advertisements in the newspaper or electronically-generated phone calls or a website. Finally, determine how both advertisements will be shared: on TV? On the radio? At a rally? Online? Remember, you want to reach the most voters!

Create a motto or slogan to encourage people to vote. Design and create two advertisement tactics to get the word out. Then, explain how each tactic will help improve voter turnout in your area.

SO-AND-SO'S DAY

Many holidays are celebrated to honor certain people. You feel a certain person from history deserves this special recognition as well. Maybe it is a current or former politician. Maybe it is an ancient ruler. Maybe it is someone who is involved in service work around the world. Maybe it is someone who has made a famous discovery.

Find out everything you can about this special person. Write a letter to the government to persuade them that this person deserves his or her own holiday. In your letter, include two or more reasons why this person should have a special day devoted just to him or her. Be persuasive! Explain how this new holiday will bring a new awareness of this person's contributions to history and/or society and why this is important.

POSTCARDS FROM AGO

People make new discoveries all the time. Some discoveries let us get a new glimpse of what life was like long ago. These findings are thrilling to history lovers! As a matter of fact, an historian has just unearthed a time capsule of sorts. In it were several objects and three postcards detailing life during a certain time period.

Put together a collection of objects that may have been included in this time period. (Illustrate the objects if you cannot find them or make models of them.) Also, write summaries explaining the significance of each object. Place the objects and summaries in a shoe box, clear plastic jar, or bottle.

Use note cards to make postcards. Draw pictures on the blank side showing important people, places, or events from this time period. Then, write letters on the back addressed to people in the future. Explain why the illustrated people, places, or events are important.

CHAPTER EIGHT

Rubrics for Evaluating Student Work

One essential component of any unit plan includes a process, strategy, or system for determining the level of students' proficiency with regard to the skills and information they were to have learned from instruction. In other words, how will you evaluate students' understanding, and how will you grade them? This idea was discussed to some extent in the previous chapter when differentiating between formative (informal) and summative (formal) assessments. Some evaluation strategies, such as tests and quizzes, naturally lend themselves to quantifying student achievement. Each question is worth so many points, which add up to a certain percentage grade. Most writing assignments, however, are much more subjective in nature. To this author, the most unfair practice a teacher can hold is to assign a written task to students without having considered how it will be used to evaluate student understanding or its value toward an overall grade.

One approach to evaluating students' written work more objectively is to pair them with rubrics, rating scales, or checklists. Although these three evaluation techniques are similar, each serves a slightly different purpose, and each provides a different level of specificity in the evaluation of student work.

Assessment Strategy 1: Rubrics vs. Rating Scales vs. Checklists

Rubrics, rating scales, and checklists are some of the ways teachers can evaluate (or grade) student work. A rubric is very detailed. It tells students the exact elements that matter the most in their project, and it defines the exact criteria related to the quality of the work that will be used in the evaluation. The **Research Report Rubric** on page 94 is an example of a rubric.

A rating scale is a modified rubric. It is less specific regarding the quality of each criterion being evaluated. The **Project or Problem Rating Scale** on page 96 is an example of a rating scale. The criteria for evaluating student work mirrors what students might see in a rubric, but the scale is less specific, more subjective, and less definitive.

Checklists are simple lists of tasks to review, and they receive a yes/no response or a check if completed. These are useful for students to self-evaluate their work prior to submitting it for review. The **Project Completion Checklist** on page 97 is an example of a checklist. Some teachers assign numeric quantities to each criterion, depending on its importance, and use this score as part of the overall evaluation of the student's grade.

When assigning larger tasks that are best evaluated using rubrics or rating scales, be sure to distribute the evaluation criteria at the onset of the project. Review the criteria with the class. Be sure everyone is clear and has a record of how the work will be graded. If possible, leave room for student and teacher comments regarding the work in progress as well as the final product.

Assessment Strategy 2: Effective Feedback

One critical element to the completion of projects is the use of regular feedback. Susan Brookhart (2008) suggests making "as many opportunities as you can to give students positive messages about how they are doing relative to the learning targets and what might be useful to do next" (p. 59). This might be accomplished through small-group feedback, whole-class feedback, or individual feedback, depending on the instructional level of students and the skill appropriateness of the task. Assigning a project and setting a due date with no communication in between leaves students wondering, questioning, and worrying over whether they are on the right track or whether their project will meet with your approval. This is the part of social studies that most closely mirrors a language arts class. In language arts, students are likely learning the process of writing: brainstorming, drafting, revising, editing, and publishing. You, however, are the social studies teacher. Your students are learning about wars, world events, and Washington. Longer projects are valuable learning and assessment tools. Many students enjoy them, and teachers can have a tremendous sense of accomplishment regarding their social studies instruction when they see the exemplary work coming back to them from their students in this fashion. For optimal work, students need regular feedback. So, how do you provide the language arts (writing process) support students need when you are not a writing teacher?

First, you might try collaborating with the language arts teachers. Let them know about your project ahead of time, and ask their opinion of the task. Perhaps they will offer suggestions that will really elevate the interest, rigor, and relevance of the project. Then, have them review the evaluation criteria you plan to use or ask them for a rubric they use. This is an opportunity for you to hold students accountable for what they have been learning in language arts and have them apply it in a report. The language arts teachers will thank you! Hopefully, they will offer (if not, you can suggest it) to provide feedback to the students as they complete their projects. They might also have suggestions for providing time for feedback during class that will not intrude fully on your class time.

Another option for providing regular feedback is to be available before or after school for students or to arrange time during the school day when they might stop by to see you. If daytime is not possible, students can post their projects to a secure blog or website, or they can email it to you at different stages of completion. You can then access students' work any time from any computer, include suggestions for changes, or post positive and encouraging comments to keep students motivated and interested.

Finally, peer review is another viable and useful option for providing regular feedback to students. When time is short, students can pair up to take on the roles of listener/observer and sharer and offer thoughtful feedback to the students doing the sharing. Do not assume that students know how to do this. A little time spent early in the school year modeling and practicing effective feedback will save time in the long run. Consider that you are just one person. To meet with twenty-five students individually in a fifty-minute period, each student has the benefit of your ear for an average of just two minutes. However, if students are paired or put in small groups to give/receive feedback, each student could have up to five full minutes to share his or her progress with a partner. Once both partners have had a chance to share, only ten minutes of class time have been used for this purpose, leaving a full forty minutes to continue with instruction. Your language arts professionals may have additional suggestions for developing a classroom environment that promotes positive peer feedback. Use their skills and talents to your advantage to get the most out of your instructional time for the overall benefit of student learning.

Assessment Option 1: Research Report Rubric

	4	3	2	1
Topic or Concept	Topic is relevant to a recent unit of study and has tremendous value as a research project; topic sentence has value to today's reader	Topic is relevant to a recent unit of study and has some value as a research project; topic sentence has value to today's reader but may be unclear	Topic may be relevant to a recent unit of study and has limited value as a research project; topic sentence may have value to today's reader but is unclear	Topic irrelevant to a recent unit of study and has little value as a research project; unclear or no topic sentence
Sources	Student utilized highly appropriate and reliable sources: books, journals, and electronic sources	Student utilized appropriate and reliable sources: books, journals, and electronic sources	Student utilized at least one appropriate or reliable source: book, journal, or electronic source	Student utilized inappropriate or unreliable sources: books, journals, or electronic sources
Organization of Content	Report is well organized with a clear beginning, middle, and end	Report is organized with a beginning, middle, and end, but some content may be misplaced	Report may be organized with a beginning, middle, or end but not all three	Report is unorganized with no clear beginning, middle, or end
Details	Supporting information is clearly and directly related to each main point; details offer substantial support of main ideas	Supporting information is mostly clear and directly related to each main point; details offer strong support of main ideas	Supporting information may be unclear or indirectly related to each main point; details offer limited support of main ideas	Supporting information is unclear and indirectly related to each main point; details offer little to no support of main ideas
Vocabulary	Report uses substantial, highly specific scientific vocabulary	Report uses adequate specific scientific vocabulary	Report uses some specific scientific vocabulary	Report uses little to no specific scientific vocabulary
Ancillaries	Report includes adequate charts, diagrams, photos, illustrations, or other supporting features directly related to the text	Report includes charts, diagrams, photos, illustrations, or other supporting features related to the text, but some may be unclear	Report includes at least one: chart, diagram, photo, illustration, or other supporting feature related to the text	Report has no charts, diagrams, photos, illustrations, or other supporting features related to the text
Overall Review	Report is complete and thorough; it is written neatly with mostly correct grammar, punctuation, and spelling	Report is complete but not fully thorough; it is mostly neat with mostly correct grammar, punctuation, and spelling	Report is incomplete or not fully thorough; it lacks neatness and has some incorrect grammar, punctuation, and spelling	Report is incomplete and not thorough; it lacks neatness and has incorrect grammar, punctuation, and spelling

TOTAL: _____ / 28

Teacher Comments:

Assessment Option 2: Prompt Rubric

Title _____

Name _____ Period _____

	4 Outstanding	**3** Good	**2** Fair	**1** Needs Work
TOPIC	Writing is on topic from start to finish.	Writing is on topic, but lacks coherency.	Writing is somewhat on topic, but lapses occur.	Writing is not on topic.
CONTENT	Writing has ample details, vivid descriptions, and specific vocabulary.	Writing has some supportive details, adequate descriptions, and/or mostly specific vocabulary.	Writing has few details that may not support the main ideas, few (if any) descriptions, and some unspecific vocabulary.	Writing lacks any supportive details, descriptions, and/or specific vocabulary.
ORGANIZATION	Writing is well organized.	Writing is somewhat organized.	Writing has little organization.	Writing lacks any organization.
THOROUGHNESS	Writing is complete and thorough.	Writing is mostly complete but may not be fully thorough.	Writing is somewhat complete, but lacks thoroughness.	Writing is incomplete and not thorough.
CONVENTIONS	Writing includes correct grammar, spelling, and punctuation.	Writing includes mostly correct grammar, spelling, and punctuation.	Writing includes incorrect grammar, spelling, and punctuation.	Very little grammar, spelling, and punctuation are correct.

TOTAL: _____ / 20

Teacher Comments:

Assessment Option 3: Project or Problem Rating Scale

Project Title: Student:	0 Not there	1 Attempts	2 Good	3 Strong	4 Outstanding	TOTAL
Project completed following directions						
Includes						
Writing is appropriate to format						
Correct grammar, spelling, and punctuation						
Writing demonstrates understanding of social studies concept						
Overall impression						

TOTAL: _____ / 24

Positives:

One area to improve:

Assessment Option 4: Project Completion Checklist for Students

Project Completion Checklist

Directions: Review the directions for the research project. Use this checklist as a self-evaluation to determine whether you are ready to turn in your project.

Report Content

☐ My project has a clear beginning, middle, and end.

☐ I have something great to say. My main idea is clear. It is stated in the introduction and conclusion.

☐ My details are directly related to, and supportive of, the main idea.

☐ My project moves easily from one idea to the next. I used appropriate and varied transitions.

☐ Each paragraph has a topic sentence and supporting details.

☐ The vocabulary I use is specific and precise.

☐ I include just enough charts, diagrams, or illustrations to support the content. They are labeled with captions, and their purpose is clear.

☐ All grammar, spelling, and punctuation are correct.

Just the Facts

☐ I use facts and evidence, not opinions, when completing my work.

☐ I used two or more reliable sources to find facts and information.

☐ My list of sources is complete.

Overall

☐ My work is my own. I use my own words and stay true to my own ideas.

☐ My project reflects my writing style.

☐ My project is interesting to read.

Something I had trouble with was: _____

_____

_____

I (circle one):   DID   DID NOT   enjoy this assignment because:

_____

_____

_____

Azzam, A. "Clash! The World of Debate." *Educational Leadership*. Vol. 65, No. 5, 2008.

Bellanca, J. *A Guide to Graphic Organizers*. Thousand Oaks, CA: Corwin Press, 2007.

Brookhart, S. M. "Feedback that Fits." *Educational Leadership*. Vol. 65, No. 4, 2008.

Common Core State Standards Initiative. Introduction, English Language Arts Standards.

Retrieved from www.corestandards.org/the-standards/english-language-arts-standards, 2010.

Drapeau, P. *Great Teaching with Graphic Organizers*. New York, NY: Scholastic, Inc., 1998.

"Freeology," http://freeology.com/graphicorgs (accessed July 20, 2011).

Godin, D. *Amazing Hands-on Literature Projects for Secondary Students*. Gainesville, FL: Maupin House Publishing, 2010.

"Glogster EDU," http://edu.glogster.com (accessed July 20, 2011).

"Google Docs Tour," www.google.com/google-d-s/tour1.html (accessed July 20, 2011).

Harvey, S. *Non-fiction Matters: Reading, Writing, and Research in Grades 3-8*. Portland, ME: Stenhouse Publishers, 1998.

"Historical Inquiry Project," www.historicalinquiry.com. Doolittle, P., Hicks, D., and Ewing, T. Virginia Tech, 2005.

"History Channel for the Classroom," www.history.com/shows/classroom (accessed July 20, 2011).

Hunter, M. *Mastery Teaching*. Thousand Oaks, CA: Corwin Press, Inc, 1982.

Iasevoli, B. "A Nation at War" from *Time for Kids* online, www.timeforkids.com/TFK/teachers/wr/article/0,27972,2061566,00.html. April 1, 2011: vol. 16 no. 21.

"Intodit.com," www.intodit.com (accessed July 20, 2011).

Just Read Now: Frayer Model. "Just Read Now!," www.justreadnow.com/strategies/frayer.htm (accessed July 20, 2011).

Kidspiration and *Inspiration* software are trademarks of Inspiration Software, Inc., 9400 SW Beaverton-Hillsdale Hwy., Suite 300, Beaverton, OR, 97005. (503) 297-3004.

"Library of Congress," www.loc.gov/index.html (accessed July 20, 2011).

March, T. "Searching for China: WebQuest," 1995. http://tommarch.com/learning/ChinaWebQuest1.html (accessed July 20, 2011).

Marzano, R. *Classroom Instruction that Works*. Alexandria, VA: Association for Supervision and Curriculum Development, 2001.

Marzano, R. *Classroom Assessment and Grading that Work*. Alexandria, VA: Association for Supervision and Curriculum Development, 2006.

McGregor, T. *Comprehension Connections: Bridges to Strategic Reading*. Portsmouth, NH: Heinemann, 2007.

McKnight, K. *The Teacher's Big Book of Graphic Organizers*. San Francisco, CA: Jossey-Bass, 2010.

Microsoft® Office products are available from www.microsoftstore.com.

"National Archives," www.archives.gov (accessed July 20, 2011).

National Archives, The. "Powers of Persuasion, Poster Art from WWII." www.archives.gov/exhibits/powers_of_persuasion/powers_of_persuasion_intro.html (accessed July 20, 2011).

National Geographic Kids Magazine is available for purchase: "National Geographic Subscriptions," National Geographic. www.natgeomagazines.com (accessed July 20, 2011).

Pauk, W. and Owens, R. J. Q. *How to Study in College (10th ed.)*. Independence, KY: Cengage Learning, 2010 [1962].

Reeves, D. *Ahead of the Curve: The Power of Assessment to Transform Teaching and Learning*. Bloomington, IN: Solution Tree, 2007.

Report of the National Commission on Writing in America's Schools and Colleges. *The Neglected "R": A need for a writing revolution.* The College Entrance Examination Board, April 2003.

Report of the National Commission on Writing in America's Schools and Colleges. *Writing: A Ticket to Work...Or a Ticket Out. A Survey of Business Leaders.* The College Entrance Examination Board, September 2004.

Rowntree, D. *Learn how to study*. London: Macdonald and Jane's, 1976.

"Scribblar," www.scribblar.com (accessed July 20, 2011).

Simmons, K. and Guinn, C. *Bookbag of the Bag Ladies Best*. Gainesville, FL: Maupin House Publishing, 2000.

"Teachers' Domain," www.teachersdomain.org (accessed July 20, 2011).

Time for Kids, www.timeforkids.com/TFK/ (accessed July 20, 2011).

"Twitter," http://twitter.com/ (accessed July 20, 2011).

Wagner, T. "Rigor Redefined." *Educational Leadership*. Vol. 66, No. 2, October 2008.

Wiggins, G. *Educative Assessment: Designing Assessments to Inform and Improve Student Performance*. San Fransisco, CA: Jossey-Bass, 1998.

"Wikispaces." www.wikispaces.com (accessed July 20, 2011).